The Inclusion Breakthrough

Praise for *The Inclusion Breakthrough*

"*The Inclusion Breakthrough* provides a practical framework for how organizations can truly leverage diversity as part of the business strategy, rather than as an add-on program. Fred and Judith's proven methodology and real world examples definitely serve as a roadmap to achieving breakthroughs in organizational performance."

Richard Chang, CEO, Richard Chang Associates, Inc.
and author of The Passion Plan and The Passion Plan at Work

"Breakthrough is not too strong a word for what Fred and Judith have achieved here. They actually explain how to create a culture of inclusiveness for today's and tomorrow's competitive world. As always from these two authors, a state-of-the-art book."

Peter B. Vaill, Professor
University of St. Thomas

"In this stupendous book, Fred and Judith have unlocked the secret to success in this fast changing global economy. Their combined 50+ years of experience working with the best companies in the world gives them a unique perspective on how to create lasting change. Their methodology works! Every senior executive, manager, and change leader would benefit from reading this book and using the methodology presented."

Ava Albert Schnidman, Partner
Deltech Consulting Group, Ltd

"At a time when events have caused some people to see differences as a threat, it is critical that we stop looking at diversity as an issue separate from how we run our businesses. *The Inclusion Breakthrough* goes beyond the typical call to change attitudes and gives business leaders practical examples of practices, policies, and procedures that have been used successfully to make positive change."

John W. Coné, former VP of Learning
Dell Computer Corporation

The Inclusion Breakthrough

—————•—————

Unleashing the Real Power of Diversity

Frederick A. Miller & Judith H. Katz

BK

BERRETT-KOEHLER PUBLISHERS, INC.
San Francisco

Berrett-Koehler Publishers, Inc.
235 Montgomery Street, Suite 650
San Francisco, CA 94104-2916
Tel: (415) 288-0260   Fax: (415) 362-2512   www.bkconnection.com

Ordering Information

Quantity sales. Special discounts are available on quantity purchases by corporations, associations, and others. For details, contact the "Special Sales Department" at the Berrett-Koehler address above.

Individual sales. Berrett-Koehler publications are available through most bookstores. They can also be ordered direct from Berrett-Koehler: Tel: (800) 929-2929; Fax: (802) 864-7626; www.bkconnection.com

Orders for college textbook/course adoption use. Please contact Berrett-Koehler: Tel: (800) 929-2929; Fax: (802) 864-7626.

Orders by U.S. trade bookstores and wholesalers. Please contact Publishers Group West, 1700 Fourth Street, Berkeley, CA 94710. Tel: (510) 528-1444; Fax (510) 528-3444.

Berrett-Koehler and the BK logo are registered trademarks of Berrett-Koehler Publishers, Inc.

Printed in the United States of America

Berrett-Koehler books are printed on long-lasting acid-free paper. When it is available, we choose paper that has been manufactured by environmentally responsible processes. These may include using trees grown in sustainable forests, incorporating recycled paper, minimizing chlorine in bleaching, or recycling the energy produced at the paper mill.

Library of Congress Cataloging-in-Publication Data

Miller Frederick A., 1946-
     The inclusion breakthrough : unleashing the real power of diversity /
Frederick A. Miller and Judith H. Katz ; [foreword by Doug West].
        p. cm.
     Includes bibliographical references and index.
     ISBN 1-57675-139-2
     1.Diversity in the workplace. 1.Katz, Judith H., 1950-II. Title.

HF5549.5.M5M55 2002
658.3'008--dc21

First Edition
07 06 05 04 03 02   10 9 8 7 6 5 4 3 2 1

Book Design & Production: Jimmie Young/Tolman Creek Design • Copy Editing: Susan Pink • Indexing: Sherry Massey • Cover Design: Brian Murray

To Frederick A. Miller, Sr. (1910-1964) and Clarice Gaines Miller (1912-), parents who gave me roots and the wings to fly out of the box that was supposed to be the destiny of an inner city child born in Philadelphia, Pennsylvania in 1946 and whose birth certificate indicated "Negro." -FAM

To David B. Levine, my husband, my friend, my life partner, for the gifts of unrelenting straight talk, support of my life work, and sharing a vision of making the world different for us all. -JHK

And to all the women and men who are pioneers, champions, and allies in organizations, in appreciation of your commitment to creating workplaces that are liberating for your generation and those that follow.

Contents

—•—

Foreword by Doug West . . . . *ix*

Preface . . . . *xi*

Acknowledgments . . . . *xv*

Part 1 — The Need for an Inclusion Breakthrough *1*

Chapter One: Diversity in a Box *3*

Chapter Two: Positioning for Radical Change *25*

Part 2 — The Elements of an Inclusion Breakthrough *41*

Chapter Three: New Competencies *47*

Chapter Four: Enabling Policies and Practices *73*

Chapter Five: Leveraging a Diverse Workforce *97*

Chapter Six: Community and Social Responsibility *115*

Chapter Seven: Enhanced Value to the Marketplace *125*

Part 3 —Creating an Inclusion Breakthrough *135*

Chapter Eight: Building the Platform for Change *139*

Chapter Nine: Creating Momentum *157*

Chapter Ten: Making Diversity and
    Inclusion a Way of Life *171*

Chapter Eleven: Leveraging Learning and
    Challenging the New Status Quo *185*

Conclusion: Breaking Out of the Box *193*

Glossary *197*

References *205*

Index *207*

Foreword

———•———

Diversity and inclusion must be at the core of an organization's culture. There is no such thing as a successful "get by" diversity strategy. But for those who are willing to make the cultural change required to support an effective diversity strategy, the gains in organizational performance will be remarkable. With nearly thirty years in corporate settings, I have seen the power of diversity and inclusion, as well as the weakness of narrow cultural settings. I believe that the leaders of all organizations should be asking, "*When* will we begin to execute our diversity and inclusion strategy?" There are no "ifs" about it.

If you share these views, you know that a special and powerful synergy can exist in teams of people with wide-ranging differences. If you seek to create this synergy in your own organization, this book will be a valuable tool. Fred Miller and Judith Katz have devoted their professional lives to the principles of cultural diversity and inclusion. This book is a rich compendium of their learning and experience. I was honored when they asked me to share my perspective in this foreword.

The greatest value I can lend in this space is to underscore the authors' views on the commitments that must come from the top of any organization intent on creating a diverse and inclusive culture. The primary commitments needed from senior leaders are clear and often-repeated statements of purpose, a tight alignment of the culture change strategy with the business or organizational strategy, and demonstrated behaviors by the senior leadership team, consistent with their declarations of purpose. If any of these are missing, the result at best is what Fred and Judith call diversity in a box. At worst, weak senior commitment or a perceived lack of organizational relevance will only encourage the doubters and outright cynics.

Every organization must find its own statement of purpose in pursuing a culture of inclusion. One size does not fit all. At Toyota, our work towards creating a culture of inclusion is in harmony with and supports our vision "to become the most successful and respected car company in America." The statement of purpose must be understood to embody the larger goals and aspirations of the organization and must be communicated, communicated, and then communicated some more. Just as you begin to think you are driving everyone to distraction with your repetition, many will be hearing your commitment for the first time.

Some organizations avoid the necessary commitment to a diversity strategy because they fear it will be divisive, pitting groups or cultures against one another and alienating the dominant group with no benefit to anyone. Certainly that is a risk with any half-hearted, diversity in a box approach. And even with a well-executed effort, senior leaders must expect and endure some resistance and push back in the early stages. Every culture change initiative has its commitment-testing phase, but with a sustained clarity of purpose and perseverance, there will be an Inclusion Breakthrough. The breakthrough occurs as a result of the process of discovering, acknowledging, and valuing the differences in people. Although the process is often tough, it cannot be skipped or cut short. It is the pathway to inclusion and, by that inclusion, the pathway to all of the talent and power in your organization.

Douglas M. West
Senior Vice President and
Chief Administrative Officer
Toyota Motor Sales USA
Torrance, California
February 2002

Preface

We wrote this book because we believe in the power of diversity. Although some organizational leaders believe that they have seen and experienced the positive elements of diversity, virtually all have been practicing what we call diversity in a box. Unleashing the real potential of diversity offers performance benefits that are an order of magnitude more than most organizations have ever accomplished and many of us have ever seen.

Through traditionally restrictive policies, practices, and structures, many organizations put a blanket over people, smothering much of their diversity. We believe organizations that remove the blanket and support human diversity will be the big winners in the twenty-first century.

Many people believe that diversity is a problem that takes enormous energy to manage, address, and deal with, and that sameness is so much easier. After all, it takes work to be part of a diverse organization or team. Phil Wilson, a former executive with Oracle, had an opposite point of view. He believed that it takes more energy to keep the blanket on human diversity than to unleash it, and it takes a lot of work to maintain and deny that diversity. Diversity is natural, and any effort to stifle it takes more work than enabling it.

The real work for organizations in search of higher performance and greater success ought to be supporting diversity and aligning it for a common purpose. The real challenge for organizations is to remove that blanket.

We believe organizations are strengthened by a diversity of perspectives, nationalities, and backgrounds. We believe that all groups possess the inherent potential of diversity, but to truly leverage it you need inclusion.

- How much of themselves are people allowed and enabled to contribute?
- How are their different perspectives, talents, skills, and styles allowed and enabled to interact to create enhanced results?

This book represents what we have learned from our work over the past 30 years with a wide range of clients in a broad range of industries, from long-established manufacturing and service organizations to entrepreneurial start-ups, from Fortune 50 multinationals to non-profit foundations, from city and county governments to school districts, colleges and universities, and from individual coaching sessions to small-scale educational events to 100,000-person system-wide interventions.

Over time, what has emerged from The Kaleel Jamison Consulting Group, Inc. work is a methodology for change and creating organizational breakthroughs. This book is our effort to capture the insights, experiences, frameworks, and interventions from our decades of real-world, real-organization experiences.

Many attempts at making diversity work inside organizations have failed. We wrote this book—to help create an image of what real success can look like. In this book, we talk about what *could* be—what is available to organizations if they allow and enable themselves to flourish, to grow, and to come together and do their best work.

In our work with clients and in our service as directors on the boards of Ben and Jerry's, the Institute for Development Research, the National Training Laboratories, the Organization Development Network, the Social Venture Network, the American Society for Training and Development, and others, we have seen glimpses of what unleashing the power of diversity can do. We have seen it, we have touched it, and we have seen how much individuals, teams, and organizations have gained from it. It is hard to describe the potential we see, but we will try. *It* is the difference between black-and-white TV, color TV, and high-definition TV. When we had only black-and-white TV, most of us were satisfied. It was the invention of the century. We saw new and wonderful things. How could there be more? How could it get any better? But then color TV opened our eyes to a new reality—a new and truer view of the world. And now we have high-definition TV—multi-dimensional images, not flat people in a flat world. The world and people are more dynamic and wondrous than the earlier TV screens portrayed.

Organizations have been operating in a black-and-white TV world. They have been utilizing just one or, at most, a couple of the dimensions of humankind. They do not see or leverage the multi-dimensional diversity of humankind. They let only some people in the game and require most to conform to a very narrow bandwidth of behavior. People are more than that, and organizations *need* more than that, especially if they hope to be successful in the future. We are not saying, "Anything goes!" Far from it. We are simply saying that there is plenty of room to expand the bandwidth of appreciated and valued behaviors and styles, with an ever-present eye on whether the bandwidth serves the mission and strategies of the organization. We believe greater success awaits organizations that widen their range.

We know from experience that people have more to give than many organizations allow. In the black-and-white TV world we entered as employees in the 1960s, many people saw only a young African American man from the inner city of Philadelphia and a black college called Lincoln, and a young Jewish woman from Queens, New York, who attended Queens College. They saw a couple of dimensions and rated us on them. Many did not see the high-definition reality and potential that now has us leading a 100-plus-person consulting firm considered by many as the preeminent firm in the area of strategic culture change as it relates to leveraging diversity and inclusion. They could not imagine that those two individuals would consult to many of the Who's Who in corporate America.

Our point is that we are not exceptions. In fact, we see ourselves as normal. We are just two examples of the potential that awaits all of us if we leverage the diversity of humankind and include all people in our problem-solving and pursuit of opportunities.

We are optimistic about the future when we reflect on how little of what people have to offer, individually and collectively, has actually been leveraged by organizations. Yes, society and technology have accomplished a great deal, but we have so much further that we can go. Many organizations have achieved significant success using only a fraction of their collective experience, knowledge, and potential. We think all of us have been building, creating, and accomplishing with one hand bound behind our backs.

We believe that freeing that hand will create greatness beyond our imagination.

A note about the case studies: The examples in this book are all based on fact and experience. Details have been changed to maintain confidentiality and anonymity of organizations and individuals. In virtually all instances, the case examples do not represent isolated incidents. They were chosen because they illustrate patterns we have seen repeated consistently or solutions that have been successful in several organizations.

Acknowledgments

Fred's Acknowledgments

My first and most important acknowledgment is to Pauline Kamen Miller, the person I have been married to and built a family and a home with for the last twenty years. Thank you, Pauline, for the wonderful life we have co-created for ourselves and for enabling me to be fully the person I have needed to be, to be my best self. And, thanks to Kamen Kaleel Miller and Shay Clarice Miller for being such alive, loving, and dynamic children. Thanks for coming into our lives.

Judith H. Katz and I have been business partners since 1985 when Kaleel Jamison died of breast cancer at age 53. Judith is not just a business partner. That role and relationship does not and cannot sustain the ups and downs of working together and running a thriving consulting business for so many years. Judith is my dear friend, trusted advisor, and a pioneer in the area of racism, especially as it relates to whites. Thanks, Judith, for co-authoring this book with me and making one of my dreams come true.

. . . and we stand on the shoulders of giants who have enabled us to see beyond the valley. . .

To name a few:

Charles V. Hamilton (a great teacher and role model) and James Farmer (founder of CORE), both professors, and Stokely Carmichael (a.k.a. Kwame Toure), adjunct faculty at Lincoln University, Pennsylvania, in the 1960s when I learned from them about life, being black, and social change.

And other pioneers: Henry Morgan (Polaroid, Boston University, and Ben and Jerry's), Kaleel Jamison (dear and missed friend, colleague, boss, and "big sister"), Henry Roberts (CEO of Connecticut

General Life Insurance Company while I was an employee from 1968 to 1979), Rick Kremer (a partner in "crime"/change at Connecticut General Life Insurance Company), Edie Seashore (a friend, mentor, consultant to KJCG, and great woman), Dick Gregory and Malcolm X. Giants all. Thank you for touching my life and teaching me so much.

Judith's Acknowledgments

I am deeply indebted to many individuals. First and foremost, I want to thank my parents Ilse and Bill Katz, who raised me with a set of values, vision, and passion about addressing injustice in this world. They helped instill in me an understanding that as a white, Jewish woman I had to play a role for change.

Additionally, I am appreciative and thankful to our clients and internal partners: Barbara Arnold, Capers Brown, June Cohen, Fred DePerez, Keith Earley, Claude Elsen, Dory Gasorek, Danny Grossman, Miles King, Karon Moore, Barbara Patocka, Ron Wesson, Doug West, Clarence Wilson, and Phil Wilson, to name a few, who have been willing to put their faith and trust in me and us and embark on a breakthrough journey. It is through these partnerships that I have been tested and strengthened.

To Bailey Jackson, a dear friend, colleague, and supporter, who is one of the preeminent thinkers on social justice. Bailey has helped shape our concepts and models and has always been willing to share his genius while supporting our work. Thanks.

And to David B. Levine for his insights and always challenging us to be our best.

We wrote this book with the assistance of many people. We will list only a few, and we apologize to those who we have not mentioned.

First, we want to thank all the current and past members of The Kaleel Jamison Consulting Group, Inc. (KJCG). We are privileged, honored, and inspired by our partnership, our many learnings, and your challenges for us and KJCG to be better tomorrow than today.

It is a blessing to be leaders and partners with you in the KJCG Business-Village.

This book would not have been possible without the brilliance and hard work of Caryn Cook. Thank you, Caryn, for your dedication and involvement. Your leadership, guidance, and management of this project and us were way above the call of duty. We appreciate your commitment to excellence and always working to raise the bar.

Thanks to the people who assisted us in getting our words and thoughts clear and in writing: Roger Gans, Meredith Maran, Ed Kamen, Carnie Lincoln, and Pauline Kamen Miller. Thanks to Brian Murray for taking our notions of the inclusion breakthrough model and translating it into a visual model for others to understand. Thanks, too, to Diane DuBois for her assistance in supporting us every day of our lives and assisting us in making all the calls and planning the meetings that were necessary to both successfully complete this book and lead KJCG.

Of course, thoughts and concepts are just that, and sharing them in our consulting practice and with friends is communicating to a limited audience. It took someone who cares about diversity and who had a vision of the value of what we had to say to bring this book to life and into the hands of thousands of people. Thank you, Steven Piersanti and the members of Berrett-Koehler for having faith in us and this project.

PART ONE

The Need for an Inclusion Breakthrough

Organizations today are being forced to live by their wits. Their survival depends on their ability to out-think their competition, which can only be accomplished by catalyzing the intellectual resources of their people into creative new solutions. A single person's brilliance or a single group's point of view is no longer enough to sustain an organization's growth in the face of global competition. Tomorrow's successful organizations will be those that harness the collective and synergistic brilliance of all their people, not just an elite few. The stock-market stars will be the organizations that capitalize on the diversity of their workforce.

But capitalizing on diversity requires more than simply hiring a diverse workforce. Radical changes are needed also in both the structure and culture of most organizations—in their policies and practices, the skills and styles of their leaders, and the day-to-day interactions among all their people.

1

Many organizations will fail to make these changes because the changes seem too radical. Those organizations will not survive. To many people and most organizations, diversity seems like a problem, not a solution. Differences are to be avoided, not embraced and utilized. Age-old hierarchies, traditions and biases must not be questioned or examined. To make these changes to embrace and capitalize on diversity will require a true breakthrough—an *Inclusion Breakthrough*.

The first step is to ensure that diversity is seen as mission critical. When the current and future success of the organization is tied directly to the need for diversity, it becomes a powerful tool for organizational change and higher performance. Making diversity mission critical conveys its urgent nature to every person in the organization and positions the organization to reap the benefits from leveraging that diversity.

An organization that leverages diversity enables all members of its workforce to utilize their full portfolio of skills and talents. It continually seeks to broaden its diversity to take advantage of new markets, new sources of innovation, and new pathways to success.

Chapter

Diversity in a Box

Each person is a unique individual who also belongs to several different social identity groups. A wide range of differences can exist even among people who look, sound, and act alike. This *Paradox of Diversity* is a way of framing diversity that captures one's similarities and differences.

> **We are like all people:** As human beings we share similar needs and wants—to experience joy and love, to be safe, etc.

> **We are like some people:** We share culture and experience.

> **We are like no other people:** We are each unique unto ourselves.

The aspects of ourselves that are like some other people constitute our connection to specific social identity groups, those with which we share similarities, such as age or living in a particular region. But we don't necessarily identify with each group to which we belong, such as—"people with red hair" or "people who drive a Toyota convertible." Regardless of whether or not we identify with a particular group, others might put us in it because the identification has meaning to them, such as—"people who attended Cornell" or "people who live in the Bronx." Bailey Jackson was one of the first people to identify that some differences matter more than others.

3

Those that make the biggest difference are ethnicity, gender, marital status (and children), race, sexual orientation, language, physical ability, socioeconomic status, religion, and mental ability.

These differences can affect the hiring process. Many people and organizations claim they are color blind, gender blind or blind to differences. Although they consider this stance to be a positive attribute, it implies a disregard for differences. Many people have been raised to see differences as a deficit and therefore assume that differences will cease to be problematic if they are ignored.

Also, organizations that used to pride themselves on growing their own, hiring new people for only entry-level jobs and promoting from within, now find themselves needing to bring new and different talent into the organization at all levels. Many leaders have been surprised at how difficult it is to keep these new people. They are often rejected like a virus by both the organizational culture and the people who have been raised in the organization. Most "old timers" wonder why these newcomers were even brought in. The new people are never able to fit in, never able to fully participate and contribute. The organization's inability to include these new hires is often the reason for their leaving.

When a new hire is a person of color or a white woman, another issue may be played out. People often suspect that the person was hired primarily because of Affirmative Action goals to counter past discrimination. A common perception is that individuals of color or white women are hired based on lower standards or fewer qualifications and will therefore be a detriment to the organization.

These issues can be addressed by explaining a basic philosophical tenet: The intent of Affirmative Action is the hiring of competent people. The fact that Affirmative Action hires continue to be commonly perceived as "less-qualified" hires speaks to the bias that remains in many individuals and systems. Lingering in many organizations is an entrenched prejudice that can accept the promotion of some people only as being the result of Affirmative Action, rather than arising from the person's own competencies and abilities.

Another assumption about Affirmative Action that needs to be addressed is the notion that it gives an unfair advantage to certain people. For those who believe that a level playing field now exists for all involved, Affirmative Action looks like preferential treatment for particular underrepresented groups—those who have more suddenly will have less. To those who see the playing field as uneven, Affirmative Action is a means for everyone to have a chance at the opportunities.

Too often, people mistakenly use the terms Affirmative Action, Diversity and Inclusion interchangeably, reflecting the fallacy that they are equivalent. They are not. In most people's minds, diversity programs refer to people of color and women struggling to achieve a place in society. In reality, diversity is an attribute embodied in every individual.

Some organizations increase their diversity in an effort to meet Affirmative Action goals. However, this increase is superficial if the organization is not prepared to *include* an increased range of differences in its day-to-day activities and interactions.

Unfortunately, most organizations end up with a *diversity in a box* strategy. They see diversity as getting in the way of success by forcing the organization to do something it doesn't want to do. Or they see it as an issue to be managed, shaping it and getting it to "fit" in the existing structure of the organization. Still other organizations see diversity as a value and end in itself, unrelated to the mission, vision and purpose of the organization. The result: either a singular focus on representation and awareness or ignoring the issue altogether.

Regardless of the reasons why organizations begin the diversity effort, it is often thought of as an extra—a package of programs and policies run by the Human Resources or in-house training department and never tied to the bottom line. Efforts to change the representation of the organization are taken on with good intentions but are easily sidetracked or minimized when other priorities call.

When diversity is not leveraged, potential benefits to the organization and the individual are lost. For example, a Latina who is an engineer might be hired by an automotive design team to provide insight into preferences of Latinos or Latinas, while being overlooked as a potential contributor to broader engineering expertise. She ends up boxed in by her co-workers, who see her value limited to her apparent difference from the rest of the team. Her technical and design skills may not be fully recognized or utilized. Her diversity isn't fully leveraged for the common goal of the team—new and better ways of doing business. The organization loses an opportunity to tap her varied abilities and perspectives. The individual feels marginalized, leading to dissatisfaction with the work and the organization. Due to the cultural emphasis on community and higher needs for social inclusion, the impact of social exclusion is greater on many Latinos and Latinas than for people from groups that value individualism and independent action.

Hiring people of different backgrounds is no longer enough. Their presence in the organization is a start, but until it moves beyond diversity in a box, it will not unleash the full power of diversity and create fertile ground for everyone's growth in the organization and beyond.

In the current business climate, an organizational culture that *leverages diversity and builds inclusion* is essential for achieving and sustaining higher performance—and is therefore critical to an organization's long-term mission success and financial gain. This is true of international Fortune 100 companies, entrepreneurial start-ups, nonprofit organizations, government agencies, unions, and educational institutions.

When an organization leverages diversity, it sees things that cannot be seen when working from the basis of sameness. Leveraging diversity results in greater innovation and greater capacity for change. However, just *having* diversity does not result in *leveraging* diversity. Leveraging diversity taps into people's unique power and potential, thus unleashing the talent that exists.

There is a need for radical change. An organization that understands that need opens up the playing field and changes the rules of the game for success. An inclusion breakthrough is required–to leverage the diversity of all people and build an inclusive culture–because old assumptions, old styles, old approaches to problem solving and old line-ups are insufficient to help an organization survive and thrive in a turbulent environment.

An inclusion breakthrough is a process to transform the organization from a monocultural organization that values and supports sameness in style and approach, to a culture of inclusion that leverages diversity in all its many dimensions. It also is an approach for any organization that wants to transform their efforts from a diversity in a box approach to one that truly unleashes the power of diversity. An inclusion breakthrough necessitates a whole new way of life.

BARRIERS TO INCLUSION

Most organizations are filled with barriers–rigid structures, poor training processes, outmoded equipment, misguided incentive programs, and discriminatory promotion and assignment practices that keep people from contributing the full breadth of their skills, ideas, and energies to the organization's success. Expressed in conscious and unconscious behaviors, as well as routine practices, procedures, and bylaws, these barriers are typically rooted in the very culture of an organization. They favor people who are most like the founders or senior leaders of the organization. These barriers can be as invisible as air to those they favor but demeaning, discouraging, distracting, exhausting and seemingly insurmountable to those who bump up against them every day.

Barriers can be as tangible as stairways that block access to people in wheelchairs, the sign that reads MEN on the door of the only bathroom on the executive floor, or the lack of domestic partner benefits for the partners of people who are lesbian or gay. Barriers can also be subtle: being excluded from the lunch bunch or the golf outing, being seen as not ready for that leadership position, even people not hearing or remembering your ideas or name.

These barriers are reinforced by common negative beliefs about diversity and inclusion. Following are some negative beliefs:

- Differences create a barrier to higher performance because they bog down the process and lead to conflict.
- Diversity means that white men will lose.
- Only a few can succeed.
- It is too challenging to bring in people from diverse backgrounds.
- People who are different should conform.

A diversity in a box approach does not adequately address these barriers. Organizations often turn a blind eye to these barriers, only to discover that they are reinforced by a policy of diversity without inclusion.

Disadvantages of Not Including All People

Some organizations are making concerted efforts to address issues of exclusion and monoculturalism. Few, however, understand the scope of change needed. Even demographically diverse organizations often lack the basic skills and workplace environment required to leverage that diversity. In the absence of effective skills for communicating and partnering across differences, organizations tend to marginalize the people who are most different from the dominant group. These people often feel unheard, devalued, and ignored.

Without effective conflict-management skills, even organizations that are more diverse are unable to capitalize on the wealth of perspectives offered by their members. Instead of basing decisions on careful analysis and synthesis of differing viewpoints or on an informed debate on the relative merits of various people's proposals, many groups base decisions on who has the most seniority, is the most popular, or has the best track record, thereby excluding potentially significant voices and insights. Organizations without conflict-management skills may not be able to address the needs of an increasingly diverse marketplace and workforce.

For example, an advertising agency hired by one organization created two ads that were demeaning to Asian Americans. Because white people in the marketing department lacked competence and no people of color were in the group, the ad was disseminated without the organization's awareness of its offensiveness. Asian American employees and customers were upset and disappointed. At great cost and with great embarrassment, the organization was forced to pull the ads, but the damage had already occurred. This fiasco could have been avoided if the organization had acquired the competencies to understand what might be offensive.

Organizations almost always start out as exclusive, monocultural clubs (Katz & Miller, 1995). And most stay that way—even organizations that make sincere and well-meaning efforts to value diversity or become an Equal Opportunity Employer or an Affirmative Action Employer–unless an aggressive campaign is undertaken to change that condition. The people who start an organization, and then the people they hire, are usually closely matched in terms of one or more of the following: race, gender, ethnicity, age, nationality, and education. This is not an indictment. In organizations, as in life, people tend to associate with those with whom they feel most comfortable.

Although this approach might be reasonable and useful initially, its advantages fade over time. The monocultural values that result tend to reinforce a way of thinking and an approach to problem solving that may, at times, discourage people from suggesting changes, especially when anticipating the needs and wants of the leader is career-enhancing. Also, when work relationships are built upon the unwritten agreement that helping to maintain the status quo is the price of admission, causing conflict means stepping outside the relationship contract.

Extend this monocultural tendency to career advancement opportunities, mentoring and day-to-day workplace activities, and it becomes clear why most of today's organizations look the way they do, especially at the top. In the absence of specific policies, practices, and accountabilities to the contrary, most managers hire and promote the people who seem to require the least amount of maintenance. The outcome of this comfort factor is a truly remarkable statistic: Although women comprise 51 percent of the adult population of the United States and people of color comprise 40 percent (Census 2000), 95 percent of the senior leaders of businesses are white men (Equal Rights Advocates).

For many organizations, the historical belief and practice is that an efficient and successful organization requires people who fit in with and unquestioningly follow their supervisors and leaders. The age-old strategy of hiring individuals drawn from the founders' network of schoolmates, friends, colleagues, and family was acceptable and common. Today's reality makes that far too limited. The collective brainpower needed today in order to create visions beyond the abilities of one or a few requires the inclusion of people from a variety of backgrounds. The phrase "no one of us is as smart as all of us" has never been as true as it is today.

To leverage diversity for greater productivity, one organization reorganized itself into self-managed teams that were diverse in race and gender. Over a period of two years, these teams became significantly less diverse. Turnover rates were highest among the people who were least like the majority members of each group. As time went on, the diversity of the teams diminished until each team was homogenous in its race and gender. Productivity suffered as a result, with few new ideas filtering across to the organization.

This process failed because the teams didn't find the necessary support structures and accountabilities in the larger organization to effectively leverage their diversity. Members trusted only those team members they knew and associated with outside work. They tended to vote and make decisions based on what their social-network members or friends wanted or thought was best. They tended to help coworkers with whom they felt most comfortable. The team did not coalesce because people were most supportive of members of their own racial and gender group and least supportive of those outside those groups. This happened because many people found scant connection between diversity and task accomplishment. The organization's culture still supported and valued sameness and, because there was no education as to why the diversity of the teams would enable greater productivity, the teams eventually reflected the embedded and historic values of the organization. Because there were no new processes to keep the teams diverse or to help them see any benefit from diversity, they went back to what they knew best.

FLAWED FOUNDATIONS AND ASSUMPTIONS

Far too many diversity efforts fail because they are built upon a flawed underlying philosophy, strategy, or approach. One belief that some diversity programs have explicitly or implicitly built into their approach is that everything would be fine if everyone would behave like those who have historically been successful. People are encouraged to find a mentor or role model and learn from their behavior and experiences. Those who speak, look, or behave differently are sent to accent reduction or etiquette classes or are coached in performance-feedback meetings about their attitude or communication problems. This is based on the assumption that people at the top are both happy and successful, and that the goal of each individual should be to do whatever it takes to be like them.

This approach also includes the flawed assumptions that the road which led senior leaders to success is the same for people coming into the organization and that the organization and its challenges are static.

But, of course, people at the top are not always happy and not always prepared for the challenges ahead. For many, their ability to reach the top stemmed from the strong relationships they had established with others who were just like them. Because of those relationships, they were often given much latitude to struggle and fail (latitude that others—those who were so-called different—were not offered). They had people who believed in them, who did not second-guess or scrutinize their every move.

Another variation of the "be like the leaders" model aspires to assimilate those who are different from the dominant group—in United States corporations, this is usually white men. Based on the assumption that the organization is essentially fine, this strategy holds that after women of color, men of color, white women, and others outside the traditional group learn to succeed in the existing organization by behaving like the leaders—to gain equal access to hiring and promotion—all will be fine. The "be like us" attitude implies that you cannot fit in or be successful until you act like the dominant group. For most, this approach is simply not an option because their difference is their nationality, age, sexual orientation, physical ability, ethnic origin, gender, or race.

One of the biggest barriers to success for diversity efforts is the basic assumption that diversity is a problem that must be solved. This "problem-to-be-solved" approach leads to organizational blindness to the valuable resources offered by a diversity of skills, perspectives and problem-solving styles. It keeps organizations from noticing when they are actually practicing inclusion, and so impairs their ability to replicate successes, avoid mistakes, and communicate best practices to the organization as a whole. By reinforcing the message that differences are not really wanted, this approach also prevents organizations from tapping into the potential energy available to support the change process.

Some organizations build their diversity efforts around the belief that the dominant group must be torn down to build up other groups that have historically faced discrimination. As diversity programs are being instituted in organizations, the dominant group may feel that the program does not include them. They may perceive themselves being cast as the problem. They may come to believe that the only way they can be part of the solution is to get out of the way and out of the organization. The dominant group often voices concern that there is no longer a place in the organization's future for them, especially where promotions are concerned. They feel that they are being blamed for the organization's diversity-related problems. For these individuals and others, diversity leads to divisiveness. Their view is that instead of building partnerships and teamwork for higher performance, diversity tears people and the organization apart.

Some organizations make the mistake of devising a disparate smorgasbord of programs unrelated to the organization's mission, core business activities and needs. The best of these strategies read like a top-ten list of nationally benchmarked best practices, addressing such areas as training, support networks, mentoring, celebration of ethnic and cultural holidays, volunteerism, professional and career development, domestic partner benefits, telecommuting, and flextime. When performance continues to stagnate, when turnover rises, when lawsuits are filed, some organizations add another program. But until the diversity effort is understood as being mission critical and not merely diversity in a box, none of these measures will result in the desired outcome.

The motive behind the diversity effort can also doom it to failure. Some organizations implement a diversity effort based on the fact that diversity is simply the right thing to do. However, these organizations find that not everyone holds to the same moral imperative, includes the same people in groups that have been discriminated against, or believes the same volume of organizational resources should be applied to create equity. Some people fervently disagree with the need for an organization to fulfill anyone's moral imperative. Further, efforts based on a moral imperative are often abandoned when a crisis threatens the bottom line or the leaders of the moral imperative leave or change priorities.

Demographic changes in the United States and the global nature of organizations demand that leveraging diversity be considered a core success strategy. The behaviors and thinking of the past are no longer appropriate. Since the 1980s, people have been called upon to expand their behaviors and skills at an accelerated pace. No one group has a corner on the skill set for success. In fact, organizations that previously allowed entry to its middle and top levels only to people who looked and thought a certain way are now realizing that the talent required for success is found in individuals of every background. These organizations are beginning to see that the very differences people bring to the table contribute to an organization's success.

LEVELING AND RAISING THE PLAYING FIELD

Many organizations are currently involved in the difficult but crucial work of creating a more level playing field in their walls. The work is difficult because all organizations operate within the wider society, whose biases and discriminatory beliefs seep in through every crack and crevice.

Leveling the playing field allows an organization to reap the contributions of all of its people, as well as the synergies and innovations that flow from successful cross-difference partnerships and teams. However, simply seeking a level playing field is not enough. Any plan that aims only to bring the rest of the organization up to the standards applied to its dominant group is missing some fundamental factors and requirements for generating higher performance.

Because many organizations have historically treated their people as replaceable cogs or necessary overhead, the dominant group is often merely the least-abused segment of the population. When disrespecting people, including the dominant group, is standard practice, elevating everyone up to that level is not the answer.

The goal, after all, should be to create an environment in which all people are treated as irreplaceable assets. The most productive environment is the one in which *all* are enabled to do their best work and to continually improve their skills so that they can do even better work tomorrow. Organizations need higher levels of performance from everyone, not just from those who were previously under-contributing or running into barriers to their contributions.

In an environment tilted in their favor, the dominant group (again, traditionally white men) is expected not to complain or make waves. But to achieve higher performance and continuous improvement, all people must constantly challenge the status quo, examine and re-examine their processes, and become the chief operating officers of their jobs and teams. The challenge, therefore, is not to merely level the playing field, but to *raise* the field for everyone.

To level and then raise the playing field and achieve higher performance, organizations must include *everyone*. They need everyone to bring all their talents and energies to the workplace, working together to create something greater than any individual or monocultural group could do alone. An effort directed at a single group or a narrow band of groups will not create the synergy, creativity, innovation, and competitive advantage required for the highest performance and sustainability. Making the workplace more productive and rewarding for everyone in it must be a two-step process, with the two pursued simultaneously.

The first step (see Figure 1) is to level the playing field to ensure that the differences between a social identity group and the traditionally dominant group do not pose barriers to anyone's ability to do her or his best work.

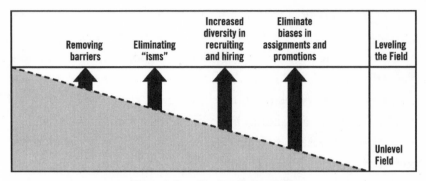

Figure 1. Leveling the playing field

The second step (see Figure 2) is to raise the entire playing field so that all people and the organization itself are equipped for maximum performance, and each person and every social identity group are leveraged as assets, resources, and organizational strengths.

Cross-difference partnership skills	Continuous individual and team development	Systems to enable all people to do their best work	Raising the Field
			Level Playing Field

Figure 2. Raising the playing field

ENABLING ALL PEOPLE TO CONTRIBUTE

A culture of inclusion requires a radical shift in thinking and operating—a new set of actions, attitudes, policies, and practices designed to enable all people to contribute their energies and talents to the organization's success. Conflict becomes constructive debate. People are sought because they are different.

Inclusion is a way of joining in a positive manner in the interest of a positive outcome, not a strategy for avoiding conflict, settling for the lowest common denominator, or assimilation. Inclusion creates a sense of belonging and when each person realizes a sense of belonging to the organizational community, motivation and morale soar.

Leveraging diversity means capitalizing on an individual's differences. An inclusive organizational culture leverages diversity by creating an environment with a broader bandwidth of acceptable styles of behavior and appearance, thereby encouraging a greater range of available paths to success. Inclusion also increases the total human energy available to the organization. People can bring far more of themselves to their jobs because they are required to suppress far less.

In fact, when individual and group differences are regarded as valued resources, as in an inclusive environment, differences no longer need to be suppressed. Those who cannot fit into the old monocultural model no longer need waste their energy trying to be what they are not, and those who can successfully suppress or hide their differences no longer need waste their energy doing so.

Only when all people, with their differences and similarities acknowledged and included, are involved in decision making, problem identification, and problem solving can the individual and collective productivity of a diverse workforce be fully engaged.

If an organization brings in new people but doesn't enable them to contribute, those new people are bound to fail, no matter how talented they are. *Diversity without inclusion does not work.*

Although the concept of diversity as an organizational imperative is spoken about at length, few management practices, policies and accountabilities have been changed to make leveraging diversity and creating a culture of inclusion a core success strategy. If they were changed, most organizations would have very different organizational landscapes. What is needed is not mere lip service to a vague business imperative, but a structured, systematic inclusion breakthrough, supported by a shared understanding that such a breakthrough is a mission-critical imperative.

COMPETING FOR AND RETAINING TALENT

To become attractive to talented people–to become a *talent magnet*—an organization must consider enhancement of its people a primary business strategy to be integrated into all day-to-day interactions, decisions and activities.

During the Industrial Revolution in the late eighteenth century, people were expected to bring their hands and feet to work. But the old assembly-line model no longer works. For organizations to be competitive today, they must inspire people to bring their brains to work too.

When an organization asks for a person's thinking, it is asking for the whole person—including the person's dreams, hopes and aspirations. This encourages each individual over time to become a knowledge worker, adding thought and value to everything she or he sees and touches. Organizations that create environments in which knowledge workers can thrive gain a competitive advantage in retaining and recruiting these valuable organizational assets. Organizations whose work environments are not as inviting may find themselves becoming training academies for their competitors. Preventing this calls for a radical change in every aspect of an organization's operations and policies.

Today's organizations are also being forced to reassess their assumptions about which talents they need most and who are their *most* valuable people. The definition of the best and brightest has changed. To meet the challenges of a global economy that is ever more focused on customized delivery of products and services, the definition of talent must be expanded to include people of different ages, genders, nationalities, colors, sexual orientations, religions, physical abilities, and other identity groups. The value of today's workforce will be measured not only by its technical skills, but also by how well individuals understand, communicate, and partner with a diverse range of customers, suppliers, colleagues, and team members.

Organizations that treat all their people as valuable resources to be nurtured, developed, recognized, and rewarded will be sought out. The constant need for fresh minds creates an interesting challenge. Over time, even organizations that have diverse work teams tend to evolve a unified point of view. Sometimes they develop a closeness that resembles exclusivity. They become too agreeable and stop questioning what is, thereby limiting their vision of *what can be.*

To ensure the ever-expanding perspective required for continuous improvement and 360-degree vision—to see around all corners and have multiple points of view for decision making and problem solving—every organization and every team in it must continuously expand its range of diversity. This effort cannot be a one-shot deal. The organization must constantly seek out, connect with, and include new dimensions of difference: lesbians and gays; people with disabilities; people of different nationalities and language groups; and on and on. It must drive the team and the organizational culture toward ever-greater inclusion. Taking the action necessary to create the workforce best able to accomplish the work of the organization cannot be viewed as a dreaded, top-down social program. It must be viewed simply as good business.

A NEW WAY OF DOING BUSINESS

Organizations are transitory entities. As the circumstances and opportunities that fueled their success fade into the past, many successful organizations come to an end. Most businesses fail in their first seven years, and in today's fast-paced environment, failure frequently happens sooner rather than later. Experts predict that 90 percent of the companies doing business today will no longer exist 20 years from now. In today's competitive environment, many organizations will not survive.

Because of the changes organizations are facing, many people and organizations are operating in crisis mode. People are postponing life-critical and life-enhancing endeavors—family, social and community obligations, vacations and sleep—in the hope that this crisis will pass. The crisis, however, will only deepen. Peter Vaill, in *Managing as a Performing Art* (1990), calls it living in "permanent white water."

What is needed is a breakthrough, and organizations are experimenting with a variety of solutions. For example, McDonald's is paying starting salaries of $30,000 for many entry-level management positions. Some companies are building Help Wanted signs right into their new buildings. Congress still argues over the minimum wage, but the issue is moot in many businesses; many entry-level people are already demanding higher pay than what is being legislated.

Without a breakthrough to keep the people that today's organizations require, declines in profitability, adaptability, resilience, and innovation await.

Organizations in search of talent are finding that the people they are looking for are, in turn, looking for a workplace that provides a welcoming environment, creates true opportunities for their professional and personal development and advancement, treats them with respect and dignity, and enables them to feel valued as contributors to the organization's success. They are looking for a place where they can affect the success of the organization and, for some, make a difference in the world.

A growing number of people are looking for workplaces that will appreciate and draw on their passions. Given the choice between comparably salaried positions, most people choose the one that offers the greatest opportunity to grow and do their best work (Stum, 1998).

The traditional organization's implied offer of a job for life did not include any promises of respect or consideration, yet demanded loyalty in return. In the emerging scenario, the organization makes no promises of longevity but instead offers respect, consideration, and opportunity in the hope of winning loyalty it can no longer demand.

A NEW HUMAN FRONTIER

Many people believe that when diversity efforts are successful and the organization changes, the only difference will be *which* group is in charge. To paraphrase Elizabeth Dodson Gray (1982) in *Patriarchy as a Conceptual Trap*: The belief that inclusion of all people is an impossibility becomes a person's "conceptual trap or limitation." We can imagine going to the moon and creating futuristic products, yet when it comes to the human condition, most people look to the past (discrimination, wars, oppression) and assume that these negative occurrences more accurately predict our future. All too often, when a diverse team is working well together, leveraging its talents and including all its members, we find ways to dismiss the possibility that this way of effectively working together can be the new norm. The creation of cultures that are truly inclusive provides the possibility of a new vision—a *new human frontier*.

IMAGINING THE POSSIBILITIES

Imagine an organization that engages people's differences as resources for creating higher performance and greater success.

Imagine an organization in which people striving to improve their ideas, products and decisions seek out collaborators who have differing points of view, backgrounds, experiences, perspectives, and ideas.

Imagine an organization whose members whistle on their way to work because they feel energized, gratified, and acknowledged on the job, they learn something new every day, and they add value through their contributions and thinking.

Imagine an organization whose senior leadership team includes a rotating group of people from all levels of the organization. This new way may seem difficult to imagine, too Pollyanna to be possible, but the fact is that inclusive behaviors and attitudes change virtually every aspect of an organization's operations.

Creating a culture of inclusion requires radical change. But the improvements that result from the change are equally radical. People must learn to work differently—every project team scans the organization to make sure it has the best and most diverse team for the job. Instead of disagreements in meetings that lead to strained compromises or avoidance, disagreements lead to better decisions based on a more complete vision of the problem and possible solutions. Work assignments are made with consideration for outside-of-work responsibilities, so people freely give their whole selves without worrying about their jobs consuming their lives. Members of the organization and customers feel loyalty to the organization because of the quality of its products and services and its social, environmental, and commercial values.

Dealing with the permanent white water in today's business climate underscores the problems organizations face to grow and prosper, and how two similar organizations can take different paths.

Two large regional banks located in urban areas, spurred on by an increasingly competitive marketplace and challenges in the banking industry, felt it crucial to address the issue of diversity. Both launched their diversity efforts with great sincerity and good intentions, each stating in nearly identical terms their commitment to being an "equal opportunity institution both for our customers and our people while maximizing shareholder values."

Bank #1 emphasized its moral imperative to become a good corporate citizen and to help improve conditions in the disadvantaged areas of its community. Bank #2 framed its effort in terms of a business imperative to expand the reach of the bank's services into new and previously underserved market areas. Then each underwent a series of mergers, followed by a period of downsizing, and their approaches took significantly different turns.

Bank #1 put its diversity effort on hold, citing organization-wide pressures that required it to "refocus on core business issues."

Staffing and branch location decisions were based on performance history. The lowest-performing people and locations were phased out. Acknowledging its moral imperative, the bank restated its commitment to continue its good corporate citizen campaign as soon as its internal situation was stabilized. Basing personnel-retention decisions on past performance, Bank #1's downsizing program adopted a decidedly last-in, first-out direction. A high percentage of its most recent hires, especially those from underrepresented social identity groups, were let go. Similarly, most branches located in low-income neighborhoods were closed.

The overall results for Bank #1, according to its public communications, were "quite satisfactory, considering the unsettled situation" from the mergers and downsizing. It retained a significant percentage of commercial lending and depositor accounts from the combined pre-merger banks and was able to serve them at reduced cost thanks to closing low-performing branches. And although its penetration into new market areas was low, improvements were expected after more stable times resumed.

Unlike Bank #1, Bank #2 continued to view its diversity effort as a business imperative throughout the merger and downsizing process. Instead of basing personnel and branch-location decisions on past performance, it based them on an assessment of their relevance to the future strategies and changing dynamics in the workforce and the community. Bank #2 strove to eliminate duplication of services and functions, while preserving resources necessary for penetrating new market areas and connecting with previously under-served constituencies.

Bank #2's pre-merger efforts had positioned it well for capitalizing on opportunities in new market areas. With judicious consolidation of branches and services in its core areas, it was able to retain a large percentage of its former business. And with its more diverse staff and advantageous locations, it was able to quickly capture a high percentage of commercial and mortgage lending, as well as private checking and deposit accounts, in previously underserved areas of its marketing region.

More than a year after the merger, Bank #1, still "committed in principle" to its moral imperative, announced another round of lay-offs as it sought to achieve "post-merger stability." Bank #2, focused firmly on its business imperative, began planning an inner-city internship and scholarship program to develop future staffing resources for its new core market areas.

The contrasting experience of these two banks is a telling example of a strategy that succeeds when it is tied to a mission-critical imperative versus the losing strategy resulting from a strictly moral imperative for initiating and implementing a diversity strategy. Although Bank #2 was forging into unknown territory with its strategy, it had much more upside potential, whereas Bank #1 used the old tried-and-true strategy common to most organizations in times of trouble.

Bank #2 embarked on an effort that represented a radical change from the way it had always conducted business—and the strategy yielded positive results. Making such a radical approach work, however, required leaders who were willing take risks and deal with resistance. Equally important, Bank #2 was willing to tie the initial, ongoing effects and opportunities related to its leveraging diversity strategy to its current and future business strategy. It integrated the effort into all activities related to its work culture, customers and business plans. It chose a path that led to greater success.

Chapter

Positioning for Radical Change

The most critical component of any effort to change culture is positioning the organization and its leaders to create and support the change. When an organization's leaders understand that leveraging diversity and building a culture of inclusion must be mission critical and that every dimension of the organization will be affected, big questions arise. "How can we make changes of this scope, intensity, and depth?" "Where do we start?" "How can we ensure success?"

In the course of answering these questions, an organization must position the effort so that leaders are leading. People take their cues from those at the top. They watch to see whether leaders believe that they have a stake in the change, whether they are investing their time and energy towards making the change and whether they are aligned with each other as they move forward with their efforts. Senior executives often do not expect the effort to require their personal involvement. However, although change can start anywhere in an organization, it can succeed only if it is led from the top. Leaders need to know how ready the organization is for change and understand its scope and boundaries. Will it encompass one division or all? Will it require a mid-course correction, an enhancement, or a total organizational change? How great a challenge will it be to enlist the support of everyone in the organization?

How senior executives perceive problems with diversity is crucial. Problems may have surfaced in the form of high turnover rates, lower-than-expected productivity, concerns regarding a lack of upward mobility raised by some social identity groups, a history of disappointing results from previous diversity training, a lawsuit, or other manifestations.

The challenges are to broaden the definition of diversity to include all social identity groups, to understand that an inclusive culture for all members of the organization is a must and to convey the links between leveraging diversity, a culture of inclusion, and organizational success.

To effectively enroll senior executives in the effort to create an inclusion breakthrough, it is vital to show them how that effort will specifically support the organization's overall goals and business strategies. When senior executives see this connection, and realize that the effort is mission critical, they can truly lead the effort and lend their voices in communicating its importance to the entire organization.

Most people worry about how diversity efforts will affect them professionally and personally. Their preconceptions must be addressed. People need to understand why the effort is important to the organization and, most importantly, what is in it for them—no matter who they are or where they are in the organization.

TOTAL CULTURE CHANGE

An organization's culture strongly influences people's behaviors and reactions. It helps determine whether people see differences of style and opinion as troublesome or as adding value, whether people are seen as overhead or assets, and whether new people are seen as potential threats or potential partners. Culture influences the way people view managers—as guardians of discipline and order or as enablers of growth and development. Culture affects the way people see change—as bad and dangerous or as good and hopeful. Culture affects also whether people want to play it safe or take risks.

For example, one organization, which was staffed mostly with economists holding advanced degrees, prided itself on its analytic nature. The culture was based on the university model. Headquarters was commonly referred to as the campus. The people placed the highest value on individuals with financial skills and economic degrees. The dominant personality was introverted; extroverts seemed out of place.

Like many universities, each department was a world unto itself, resulting in a fragmented organization that was under-leveraging its talents and capability to make decisions across functions. In this organization, few people—including senior executives, all of whom were white men—felt valued or acknowledged by their peers and managers.

In an organization like this one, in which even the traditionally dominant group feels undervalued, people who are different feel even more so. One senior leader recalled in an interview that the worst day of his life at the organization was the day he was promoted to senior vice president. When the president called him in to announce his promotion, the president mentioned that he and others were not sure that the new senior vice president was up to the challenge. They focused on what was lacking rather than on his achievements. Instead of a moment of celebration, it became a moment of self-doubt.

An atmosphere of leveraging diversity and building inclusion was needed to change this organization's culture so that all people could be treated differently—and better. The organization needed a set of more inclusive competencies for interacting and working together. Its management practices needed to change from a dressed-up version of command and control to a style that would maximize the talents of all members of the workforce. People-related policies and practices needed to be tied to the organization's current and future business challenges and opportunities. Finally, like other major organizational strategies, the change effort needed to be led and modeled from the top.

After two years of consultation, education, and systems changes, the culture began to change. It became the norm to open meetings with thank-yous to people who had made important contributions. Also, the size and composition of the top leadership group expanded. No longer was one social identity group or profession perceived as one-up compared to others. As the organization began to see and appreciate a broader group of people, a more diverse group of stars started filling the pipeline and moving into senior positions.

For an organization's culture change effort to succeed, its leaders must know how much effort will be necessary. The effort must be right-sized, so that a peashooter is not used to dismantle a boulder.

MAKING HIGH PERFORMANCE A WAY OF LIFE

When the organization recognizes that leveraging diversity and inclusion is crucial to its overall success, it moves the effort from a loose collection of best practices to an organizational strategy to improve performance. It becomes a *way of life* in the organization. The model in Figure 3 outlines that journey through five levels of development.

Level one: Developing individual awareness

Many organizations currently involved in diversity-related activities are doing diversity in a box. Their diversity activities are pre-packaged, one-size-fits-all training exercises strictly relating to differences between people. The focus is often primarily on race and gender differences. Some add differences in sexual orientation, personal style, physical ability, or nationality. The goal of the work

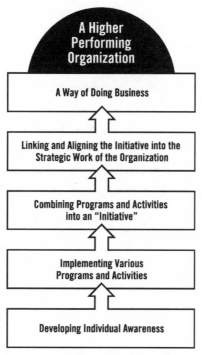

A Higher Performing Organization

A Way of Doing Business

Linking and Aligning the Initiative into the Strategic Work of the Organization

Combining Programs and Activities into an "Initiative"

Implementing Various Programs and Activities

Developing Individual Awareness

Figure 3. The way of life model

is to help people from the dominant culture better understand people from other cultures or social identity groups.

The implied benefit and desired outcome is to change the way people see difference. To do this kind of diversity work, organizations primarily use awareness education programs, ranging in length from a few hours to a few days, coupled with cultural events such as Ethnic Food Lunches, Diversity Days and Culture Celebration months. These activities are designed to increase individual awareness, sensitivity, and understanding of other cultures, but they are only the beginning of a true education about diversity and inclusion, and sometimes a flawed one. The lessons from these events are often piecemeal generalizations and abstractions about groups rather than opportunities for direct contact with people who are different. Learning tends to be intellectual rather than experiential, leaving people with perhaps a more thorough knowledge of group stereotypes but no practical skills for communicating or partnering across differences.

Level two: Implementing various diversity and inclusion programs and activities

Sometimes an initial awareness about diversity issues leads to the understanding that more work is required. At this point, organizations may institute additional programs, such as mentoring, support networks, high-potential career development, and targeted recruiting.

When implementing multiple programmatic interventions, organizations often select a menu of programs from different vendors or decide on programs based on benchmarking studies, each focusing on a specific diversity issue. Although the programs may be coordinated through the same department or committee, they remain loosely related at best.

Level three: Combining programs and activities into an initiative

When an organization realizes that its future success hinges on its capability to achieve higher performance through leveraging diversity and inclusion, the diversity work that had been given piecemeal attention as a soft, people-related pursuit becomes a business priority.

The various elements of the diversity work are evaluated, and those activities that fit with the strategic intent of the organization are knitted together into a diversity initiative. The investment in this initiative is justified through the creation of an organizational imperative or business case. Such a shift is based on a comprehensive diagnosis of the interrelationship of three key areas: high performance, leveraging diversity, and a culture of inclusion. A comprehensive strategy is developed, including time frames, accountabilities, and the requisite resources to achieve the strategic goals.

The investment also includes changes in people-related systems, management practices, and accountabilities. The focus moves from the needs of individuals to the needs of the entire system, as well as the need to create new competencies for a new culture and workplace.

Level four: Linking and aligning the initiatives into the strategic work of the organization

For maximum effectiveness in changing people's behaviors and enhancing organizational outcomes, an organization must integrate leveraging diversity and inclusion into the strategic work and goals of the organization. This means integrating new competencies and practices into all of the organization's other major strategies and initiatives: leadership, quality, mergers and acquisitions, strategic alliances, downsizing, or re-engineering.

Level five: A way of doing business

As an organization unleashes the synergies gained from integrating its leveraging diversity and inclusion efforts with its strategic goals, it can measure the benefits in new or improved processes and outcomes. Institutionalizing the change involves using these and other measurements to create accountability among senior executives, managers, and all members of the organization. Everyone in the organization needs to acquire, practice, and improve their grasp of these new competencies, thereby enhancing the organization's skill base, culture, overall performance, and organizational success.

IS IT ONLY MARKETING HYPE?

Although it had researched and instituted the best diversity practices available, Organization A was charged with racial discrimination and faced the possibility of a major class-action lawsuit.

The executives of Organization A had adopted practices to increase and support diversity based on the methods of other organizations in hopes that the practices would create a more equitable work environment. The organization's leaders prided themselves on having created a meritocracy. They felt confident that in recent years the organization had been changing its diversity practices for the better. They had performed well in recruiting and hiring a diverse work-force. Their immediate challenge was to ensure that the diverse popula-tion stayed and was progressing upward through the organization.

Over the years, Organization A had slowly built up a small cohort of senior white women, and senior executives were feeling pretty good about that. But to the surprise and great disappointment of the senior executives—95 percent of whom were white men—over an 18-month period, most of the white women left. The pipeline was getting narrower.

At first, the executives were unwilling to see or acknowledge that systemic issues were causing the problem, despite the fact that there were other indicators of organizational problems. For example, racist graffiti had been appearing on conference room walls. In response, the leaders had cameras mounted and issued additional security checks throughout the building. The racist graffiti stopped, and the surface calm was restored. They adopted other practices to correct what they saw as minor bumps on their path to greater diver-sity. Their efforts included employee networks, a mentoring pro-gram, and a one-day training session to increase awareness of equal employment opportunities.

In the meantime, organizational-effectiveness surveys showed that people felt that there was no consistency in the application of management policies and that promotions were neither fair nor based on merit. People did not trust their managers or their co-workers; managers were not always honest with their people. Avoiding issues and being political was more important than "straight talk" (Jamison, 1985). Everyone, including the managers, acknowledged that they had poor management and people skills and an inability to deal with conflict. The managers acknowledged also that diversity in the workplace was new to them and they felt ill pre-pared to deal with it.

Even with all the actions and programs that the organization had undertaken, little had substantively changed. Women in the organization continued to leave. The Director of Diversity realized that the organization's efforts to date were neither changing the culture nor showing the senior executives and other managers that what seemed to be isolated incidents were actually symptoms of bigger and more systemic problems. The top executives saw no direct connection between the diversity effort and the direction of the business.

In spite of all this, the organization was profitable. Many long-term managers believed that the organization was basically sound and that people would succeed if they would only learn to fit in and acquire the necessary tools.

When the survey and interview data was presented to the organization's leadership, the costs and benefits of creating a culture of inclusion became clear. The organization's current profitability was not because of its traditional management practices and culture but in spite of them. Many people in the organization, white men included, felt stifled by strict chain-of-command communications and hierarchy. People with potentially profitable new ideas and entrepreneurial spirit were seeing more opportunities outside the organization than inside. Instead of a human-resource and public relations centered issue, the organization's leadership recognized building a culture of inclusion as the key for future growth.

As a result, the organization initiated a comprehensive strategy of culture change that placed leveraging diversity and inclusion as its centerpiece. It became clear to the leadership of Organization A that in these days of ever-increasing competition, pursuing every opportunity for success is critical. They also saw that a culture of inclusion that leverages diversity represents just such an opportunity.

ALIGNING CULTURE CHANGE
WITH THE MISSION

It is almost impossible to create an inclusion breakthrough if the organization fails to link and integrate its strategic initiatives with its mission, vision, values, external environment, people systems, and management practices. The alignment of all of these key elements creates synergies that are far more productive than the sum of the parts. This is an important prerequisite for achieving higher performance. After this alignment has been accomplished, the organization gains the potential inherent in leveraging diversity and the culture of inclusion.

However, *higher performance cannot be achieved without the right people.* The organization first needs a strategy for retaining and obtaining the people with the right talent and mix of skills. Many organizations have those people today, but too many leaders brag about having the best and brightest people, while they treat them as if they are the wrong people. These people must be treated with respect so they are able to do their best work.

EDUCATING LEADERS ABOUT THE CHANGE

Any change effort must be grounded in a comprehensive understanding of the organization's current state. To have a true picture of the challenges and opportunities in the marketplace and to utilize the full capabilities of the workforce, senior leaders must know that they are embarking on an organizational and personal development journey. They must be committed to meeting the challenges this effort will pose for them and for everyone else in the organization.

To be positioned for change, senior leaders must be ready to:

- Acknowledge the level of dissatisfaction with the current state of the organization

- Recognize the critical reasons why organizational and personal change is needed

- Identify and support individuals who are advocates for change and are willing to be the pioneers for the new culture

Senior leaders come to know the truth—or at least gain a new perspective on differences in the organization—in various ways, such as when the organization finds itself facing litigation; when a family member marries or adopts a child of another religion or race; or when they develop a close professional relationship with someone who is different from them along some dimension of diversity. Sometimes organizational issues strike home personally. For example, several senior leaders at one organization began hearing from their daughters about the stereotyping, biases, and limitations they experienced in their jobs. This caused the leaders to develop a new understanding and to wonder if those same biases were occurring in their own organizations.

A data-collection process offers an open window to those in the organization who often do not get heard and to the challenges and opportunities that may be keeping those people from fully leveraging their talents. When based on focus groups (which divide members of the organization into homogenous groups) and questionnaires completed by a significant portion of the population, the data-collection process can be a powerful intervention. It can raise critical issues and send a signal that the organization is interested in listening and *changing*.

At some point in the journey, senior leaders may engage in an educational experience in which a diverse group of individuals is invited in as partners to share, in a direct and personal way, the different experiences that people in the organization are having. These educational sessions can be powerful. Leaders can learn what life is like for some people who are succeeding despite the many barriers that they experience in the workplace.

CREATING A SAFE ENVIRONMENT

One aspect of the organization's culture that must be addressed is safety. Creating a safe environment for all is a challenging task because it requires some people to change behaviors that they see as personal choice: "I have a right to talk any way I want." "You can't tell me who to like." "Why should I have to change? I've been acting this way long before 'they' arrived." "Why do I have to hire people I don't think will be successful here?"

It is easy for senior leaders to understand the organization's need to provide physical safety and an accident-free workplace. When they understand that safety related to diversity encompasses both physical safety (physical danger is still a serious threat for some groups, especially women and lesbians and gays) and emotional safety, they begin to grasp the magnitude of the individual and organizational change that is needed. When leaders understand that a lack of emotional safety takes a serious toll on an individual and, in turn, on the organization's productivity, the need for a culture change that creates a safe place for all will be seen as a critical foundational element in creating a culture of inclusion. Sometimes a lack of safety emerges as a fear to speak up or an unwillingness to bring ideas and perspectives to the table, even when the person sees opportunities that would benefit the organization.

Another aspect of creating a safe environment is acknowledging fears evoked by change. Fear of the unknown is a very real barrier. In most cases, resistance to an inclusion-oriented change effort is based on fears of not being included in the process and the new workplace that is being created.

Therefore, another key step in positioning the organization for an inclusion breakthrough is to build inclusion into the change process itself. The best way to free people from fear is to make them part of the planning and implementation of the change strategy. The process must be characterized by transparency: no secrets, no hidden agendas and an open communication and participation platform. *Inclusion can be built only through inclusion.*

The more people on board and the earlier they get there, the smoother the change process will be and the larger the collective wisdom available to initiate and guide the change process. Wisdom resides in every person in the organization. If the organization is to carry out its mission for its stockholders, owners, and constituents, it needs to engage that wisdom. Beginning or continuing an open and honest communication process by soliciting everyone's input sends a strong message that this is not just change as usual, and that the organization is going to be different in the future. There is no greater way to engage or empower people than to bring them into the problem-solving process and give them assignments that allow them to affect it.

People at the lower levels or fringes of an organization are often best able to see how the organization's policies, practices and strategies affect customer service, production efficiency, safety, and morale. They are often the first people to see what is *not* working. Also, people who are new to the organization bring fresh eyes and alternative ways of approaching issues and problems. They do not hold on to a "we've always done it that way" attitude that those who have been there a long time often carry. By opening lines of communication, leaders empower people at all levels to initiate change as a way of contributing to the organization's success.

Before this can happen, however, people must feel safe to speak out. They need to know that the organization is open to hearing what is really going on. They also need to be reassured that the organization will not kill the messenger and that senior leaders truly want a 360-degree view of problems to help in developing action strategies that respond to the total need.

The work environment must be made safe for discussions of tough issues, such as discrimination and lack of inclusion, as well as discussions of people's skepticism and concerns. It must be an environment that supports people as they experiment with new behaviors and make mistakes. A key to culture change is that more than the systems and policies must change—everyone must change. People must be rewarded and supported as they give up old behaviors and, through new understanding and awareness, start living new ones.

Safety is created also by a consistent effort to create a culture of inclusion that conveys to people that the effort is not a program of the month, but a well-thought-out strategy that will not be abandoned, even in the face of backlash: "It's reverse discrimination." "This is unfair." In the midst of the chaos that inevitably accompanies fundamental change, people must be able to trust that they will not end up on the wrong side of a losing battle if they learn the new competencies and start living the new behaviors. They need reassurance that they will not pay a fatal price for challenging the old ways if the organization stops supporting the new ways. Time after time, pioneers for the new end up as program-of-the-month casualties.

MAKING THE DIVERSITY STRATEGY EVERYONE'S JOB

The implementation of an inclusion breakthrough needs to happen in partnership *with* the people of the organization not *to* them. People need to see and experience inclusion as something that will benefit them, just as it benefits the organization. Leaders need to implement inclusion *with* those in the organization from day one. This makes creating an inclusive process a requirement and to do this many organizations need to change deeply ingrained historical and traditional practices.

An inclusion breakthrough strategy requires radical change at all levels. It must be interwoven into the creation and delivery of products and services. This means developing leadership and workforce competencies, as well as policies and practices that help create and support a culture of inclusion.

Externally, an organization demonstrates community and social responsibility in the way it operates. It manifests respect, acts with dignity, and provides value to the community, customers, and the marketplace. This behavior becomes self-perpetuating, thereby attracting new talent and customers, because it is delivering value and acting as a model for others to follow.

PART TWO

The Elements of an Inclusion Breakthrough

Some organizations talk about the bold actions needed to unleash the potential of their workforce and about capitalizing on diversity to deliver higher value to the marketplace. Few, however, attempt to use differences as strategic assets critical to maximizing competitive advantage. Even fewer take advantage of the opportunities diversity provides for its workforce, marketplace, community, and customers. Leveraging diversity creates the opportunity to improve everyone's performance, enhancing the organization's capability to innovate and serve all its customers and constituents and succeed in the twenty-first century.

The inclusion breakthrough cycle examines key components for leveraging diversity and creating a culture of inclusion by focusing on five key elements as shown in Figure 4:

- New competencies
- Enabling policies and practices

- Leveraging a diverse workforce

- Community and social responsibility

- Enhanced value to a diverse marketplace

New Competencies.
In most organizations, external forces affect what is required of leaders, of teams and in fact of everyone. Everyone's competencies

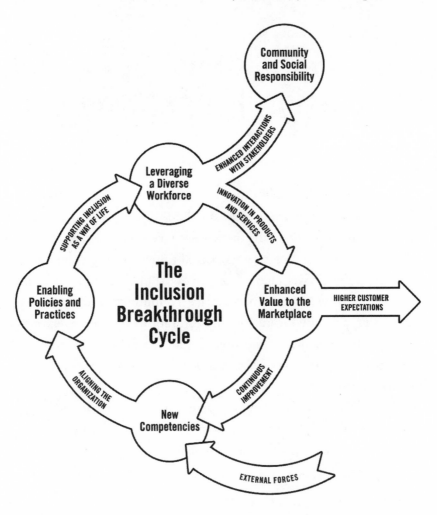

Figure 4. The inclusion breakthrough cycle

must be enhanced to enable the organization to leverage all its talent and to respond to an ever-changing and demanding environment. The skill sets needed to build a culture of inclusion must be identified, developed, and practiced. The organization needs to establish new definitions of competency for every level and every person, and then realign itself to create an environment that holds people accountable for new behaviors and competencies. Everyone needs to work to create a more inclusive culture, and everyone must be rewarded for such behaviors.

The organization needs to develop and maintain the more diverse talent base required to accomplish the organization's mission in today's world. The organization needs to develop norms that enhance innovation, problem solving and creativity so that the combined wisdom of the entire workforce is leveraged for enhanced process effectiveness and higher organizational performance. After these new behaviors are identified and developed the next step is to align the organization's policies and practices.

Enabling Policies and Practices
To sustain a culture of inclusion, an organization needs to create a new set of policies and practices that not only support new competencies but also create the environment that enables all people to do their best work. An organization's structures, both formal and informal, have a great deal to do with a person's ability to contribute. Many organizations have best practice policies but get failing marks for implementation. In too many organizations, stated and written policies are not congruent with actual practices and behaviors. Some practices to align are policies for promotions, performance management, succession planning, development opportunities, mentoring and coaching, and flexible childcare and eldercare options. Policies such as domestic partner benefits and extended parental leave also influence a person's sense of inclusion. To achieve a culture of inclusion, the bar must be raised on all policies and practices. This new baseline of inclusion supports the leveraging and unleashing of diversity.

Leveraging a Diverse Workforce

The real test of an inclusion breakthrough is *unleashing* the power of diversity by making it a way of life in the organization. The real power of diversity is found in creating a new mutualism, a new "we," that benefits both the individual and the enterprise. When an organization unleashes the power of diversity, striving for sameness and monoculturalism gives way to a more productive atmosphere of creativity and innovation. The workforce needs to become an ever-higher-performing one, comprised of partnerships and teams whose diversity works for them, not against them. Retention and recruitment efforts must develop, inspire, and enable each person, from every background and experience, to do her or his best work in service to the mission of the organization.

Community and Social Responsibility

As organizations unleash the power of diversity internally, many individuals desire to extend that energy, innovation, and learning beyond the organization to their families, the community, and other personal and professional interactions. Organizations also extend the effort beyond their walls and begin to establish true partnerships with the communities in which they operate. They need to be clear about their intent and about the values they will bring to partnerships. Organizations are affected by what is happening outside their front doors. Neighborhoods, cities, states, and nations influence an organization's success as never before. Organizations need to have a strategy to help build sustainable local and national communities in which to do business.

Many organizations are stepping up to the challenge of becoming socially responsible, both as a strategic need—to become known in the community as a good place to work, thus becoming a magnet for talent—and to be differentiated in the marketplace.

Enhanced Value to the Marketplace

Many organizations are being challenged to create new kinds of partnerships with suppliers, distributors, customers, and constituents because the marketplace and their clientele have changed. Individuals and groups that have been excluded from supplier, distributor, and customer bases for a variety of reasons in the past have now become a critical market segment. And as part of delivering enhanced value to the marketplace, organizations must be better able to engage a customer base with ever-increasing expectations about service, quality, and innovative products and advertising.

The key to having a successful breakthrough is incorporating and implementing it in an organization's overall business strategy and delivering enhanced products and services to the marketplace, customers, constituents, and other key stakeholders. One outcome of delivering enhanced value to the marketplace is that customers come to expect a new level of value, not only from the organization but from others as well. This higher expectation feeds the need for organizations to continuously improve and find more innovative solutions, products and services to meet customer needs.

And the learning process doesn't stop there. The marketplace and clientele, as well as the organization's relationship with them, trigger new strategies that the organization hadn't considered or once deemed unattainable. Thus, the circle comes around again, providing continuous learning and improvement, leading to an ongoing cycle that supports organizational readiness for change.

New Competencies

Today's organizations must function in an increasingly competitive marketplace that shifts constantly without warning or apology. Faced with intensifying global competition, organizations are being forced to perform more efficiently and effectively. They need to solve problems, execute decisions, and serve customers faster, at lower costs, and with less waste. They must improve every aspect of their organization every day. Such change cannot be incremental—it must happen quickly, and it must provide for a breakthrough in how the organization functions.

To achieve this kind of performance, organizations must avoid and eliminate the incompetence that prevents so many from doing their best work. This incompetence takes many forms, such as:

- Poor communication
- Underutilized resources
- Lack of partnership and teamwork skills
- Duplication of effort
- Fear of innovation
- Internal competition
- Working at cross-purposes

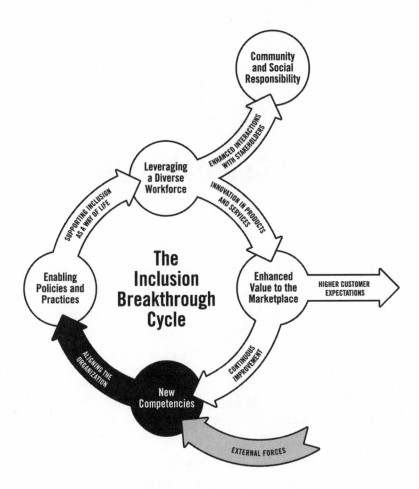

- Unmotivated workforce
- Turnover and loss of essential knowledge and skills
- Lack of collaboration across business or functional units

In this challenging environment, common sense dictates that the most successful organizations are those that maximize the combined skills of all their people. For an organization to achieve and sustain a higher level of performance, all of its components—people, processes and infrastructure—must work together, complementing and supporting each other.

People, work units, and divisions must focus on their individual tasks, working in concert up, down, across, inside, and outside the organization. For most organizations, this will require profound, fundamental, and radical change.

Few people today are Lone Rangers, working alone to accomplish their goals. Competencies such as sharing information with others, working skillfully as part of a team, problem solving collaboratively, soliciting different viewpoints, addressing and learning from conflicts and differences, and tapping into co-workers' knowledge, expertise, and talent are required.

These new work requirements go well beyond technical or functional expertise and individual ability. They extend to leveraging collective talents—enabling, engaging, and partnering with an increasingly diverse pool of people, functions and identity groups. Organizations must create and foster an environment in which each person can contribute his or her own unique perspective and portfolio of talent.

Organizations that routinely provide effective training and education in developing partnerships or teamwork skills are in the minority. Few invest in the development of leaders who can model and inspire the use of inclusive behaviors. To produce substantive, sustainable, behavioral change, an organization must invest in both the acquisition of these new competencies and in an infrastructure that supports their use. Neither alone is sufficient. It would be a waste of effort to train people to work in teams only to send them back to a workplace in which performance is evaluated exclusively on individual contributions and people must compete in a cutthroat way for bonuses, promotions, and prized special projects.

An inclusion breakthrough calls for a new sense of *we*—a sense of "we are all in this together" and "we are not all the same . . . and our differences are critical for our success." In today's organizations, new competencies are required both for leading and following, and like a computer, these competencies must be continuously upgraded and expanded just to stay current.

If they want to help bring about an inclusion breakthrough, all team leaders must learn to model behaviors and competencies for leveraging diversity and building inclusion. They must learn to communicate and partner with people from an increasingly wider range of backgrounds and job functions. They must become adept at more than simply giving orders; they must become adept also at empowering others through coaching, mentoring, delegating, supporting, cheerleading, listening, and learning from all team members.

Organization B, a large North American software company, helped fill its huge need for competent programmers by recruiting software engineers from India, Sri Lanka, and Bhutan. This meant the organization's team leaders had to develop new competencies not only for communicating and partnering with people from new countries, but also for understanding the challenges facing non-European immigrants to the United States.

To retain new recruits and enable them to contribute effectively, the software company's leaders had to learn new language skills and cultural sensitivities. As the leaders learned to partner effectively with their new Muslim, Hindu, Buddhist, and Sikh colleagues, they encountered unexpected benefits. Their new colleagues gave them insights into opportunities in their traditional domestic North American market for software, opening new domestic markets and enhancing overseas marketing as well.

As leveraging diversity becomes the means for achieving higher performance, all members of the organization—not just the leaders—must acquire competencies for building inclusion. The ability to work effectively and creatively in diverse teams and partnerships is a prerequisite for everyone's success. This requires competencies for communicating across differences, addressing and working through conflict, and creating a safe and supportive team environment, to name just a few.

For all members of the organization, these new competencies must be treated both as a valued resource and valuable currency. And like many key organizational resources, unless competencies are constantly developed and enhanced, they depreciate in value.

EXTERNAL FORCES

Organizations do not exist in a vacuum. Changes in the external environment require organizations to change and adjust their portfolios of competencies rapidly. Those external factors—new laws, regulations and industry shifts—are an invitation for organizations to do new things not only out of necessity but also to improve efficiency and the overall environment of the workplace.

At the same time, individual behaviors inside an organization do not exist in a vacuum either. When people feel safe enough to identify their needs—such as "I and others are Islamic; we require our religious practices and needs to be recognized and accommodated."—they bring a great deal of pressure upon the organization to change as rapidly as possible or risk losing them. Everyone is affected by the overall environment in the organization—the sum of its skills, education, training, written and unwritten policies, practices, physical layout, technology, competitive position, and growth rate. How an organization copes with the changes in the external environment is crucial to its survival.

WORKING IN AN INCLUSIVE WORK CULTURE

Today's organizations are facing challenges they have never had to face before, and the workforce is expecting more from them. Senior leaders, team leaders, and team members must find ways to work with people who may be quite different from them. Team leaders must figure out how to address needs and issues such as:

- Accommodating a Muslim woman who requests time off for prayer during the day

- Finding a TTD and interpreters for a man who is deaf

- Responding to people's requests to telecommute or go on a more flexible work schedule

- Addressing the concerns of single people who feel that they are asked too frequently to cover for people who have families and believe their work and personal life balance is not considered

- Communicating and working effectively with someone who has newly immigrated to the country and for whom the dominant language is not their first language

Many organizations have not caught up to these and many other new challenges. A candidate's technical or functional expertise and ability to fit in with the dominant culture continue to be the main criteria for hiring, retention and promotion in many organizations. To achieve an inclusion breakthrough, technical competence alone cannot be considered the only criteria for success.

Organizations are finding that their people cannot solve today's problems effectively by working alone. Knowledge of one's area of expertise is not enough. Leaders must manage a more diverse range of people and projects, and harness a wider set of skills. They must discard the old ways of seeing the world and doing their job to be able to yield the creativity and innovation that resides in each individual. The greater the technical and logistical complexity of a situation, the greater the need to have a breakthrough strategy that draws upon the wisdom and experience of people from different disciplines, job functions, organizational levels and cultural perspectives. It calls for harnessing similarities that people share and creating common ground and purpose among individuals, while supporting their differences as strengths.

New Definitions of Competence

Senior leaders, team leaders, and team members must possess competencies that support a culture of inclusion and translate that into higher performance. These competencies must be defined as baseline competencies—components of the mission critical imperative for enhanced leveraging of diversity and greater inclusion. Senior leaders, team leaders and team members must learn and practice specific skill sets that foster inclusive behaviors. For all people to do their best work, new competencies are required of everyone, from the mailroom to the boardroom.

Organization C was committed to creating an inclusion breakthrough and began tracking a new matrix of information to help it understand and leverage a diverse workforce. Its senior executives began looking at four key areas:

- **The diversity of the workforce:** the demographics and skill sets of the workforce at all levels

- **The inclusion of the workforce:** the hierarchy, culture and climate

- **Opportunities to grow:** development needs, project assignments, diversity of teams and positioning for future talent needs

- **Adding value:** contributions of people representing different groups and comparing potential to performance

After reviewing this information, senior executives were able to incorporate new dimensions into their assessment of team leaders, which were then used to establish baseline competencies:

- **Diversity:** Hires, promotions, turnover, pay, grade distribution, and comparisons to other organizations. Do we have the diversity needed to get the best results?

- **Inclusion:** Succession, project team diversity, cross-division and cross-department movement, mentoring, climate, morale, team effectiveness, and a "How are we doing in our treatment of you?" survey.

- **Opportunity to grow:** Training, mentoring, participation rates, and rotation assignments. Are people getting the exposure that will enable them to make larger contributions in the future?

- **Adding value:** Performance ratings and skill distribution. Do we have the skill sets we need to be successful today and tomorrow?

Incorporating new competencies—such as partnering, coaching, developing others, communicating clearly and directly, creating a supportive environment, and building an inclusive environment—is needed to achieve a mission-critical imperative. Part of an inclusion breakthrough is the need for a breakthrough in competencies—what is required of people at all levels. More than buildings, machines, proprietary patents, or technological advantages, these inclusion-building behaviors and strategies are the means by which the organization will achieve its goals.

Senior leaders must also understand that learning and practicing these skills are not just issues for others. They are, in fact, core competencies required of all leaders. Senior leaders who are committed to creating a breakthrough strategy need to recognize that they must be visible models of change. They must make clear how and why leveraging diversity and creating a culture of inclusion are mission-critical imperatives, and what will be expected at every organizational level to support and enable such a change. They must demonstrate the belief that people are core organizational assets—assets not owned by supervisors or managers but a crucial element of the equation for overall success. Senior leaders must enroll the workforce, develop a diverse leadership group, and hold themselves accountable for their own performance in their interactions with others as well as the organization's collective actions. All leaders must pursue their own development and self-awareness to be able to provide the necessary competent leadership.

Leaders must also be ready to recognize and deal with resistance that arises when making significant and radical change to long-established procedures and expectations.

At Organization D, white women on average received higher performance ratings than their white male counterparts but were not promoted as quickly. In addition, people of color, including high performers, were not promoted as often or as quickly as white men.

As part of the organization's highly publicized commitment to diversity, managers were held accountable for the diversity of their workgroups. Unfortunately, analysis of the organization's measurement and accountability practices showed that managers were rewarded only for retention of "diverse" candidates, not for their career advancement or promotion. Interviews revealed that some managers refrained from recommending their best-performing white women for promotion because they didn't want to lose them. Other managers justified their failure to recommend high-performing people of color for promotions by speculating that they might not be ready for the new assignment: "We didn't want to let them fail." Meanwhile, white men were commonly given stretch assignments.

To correct these inequities, the organization began tying a percentage of a manager's bonus to success in the development and promotion of a diverse group of people. Leveraging diversity moved from concept to reality.

Direct supervisors and managers have a great effect on an individual's work life and commitment, but so too does the individual's work group. People stay in organizations based, in part, on their connection to their colleagues. An inclusion breakthrough creates an environment in which co-workers demonstrate a commitment to each other.

If the members of the group do not have the competencies to acknowledge, support, work with, and leverage the differences that a team member brings to the workplace, all the talk and communiqués issued from the top of the organization are wasted. The workgroup can make each member's experience one of pain and tears or one of growth and creativity. The group's enhanced competencies to build a culture of inclusion that leverages diversity were a crucial factor in the success of Organization D.

One organization was striving to create an inclusion break-through and a major culture change in which people worked more collaboratively. An ongoing problem was a high degree of absen-teeism and the challenge of assigning people to work one of the three shifts.

In the past, the manager would assign individuals based on sen-iority, with some individuals getting the graveyard shift because they were new to the organization. Few people were happy with this approach, yet that was the one that had always been used.

As the organization embarked on an inclusion breakthrough strategy, one team decided that it would tackle the problem them-selves. It decided to figure out a way to cover the three shifts; address vacations, individual preferences, and needs; and work out a plan that everyone would buy into.

With much discussion, debate, and dialogue, the group members emerged with an agreed-upon schedule for the next six months. Not everyone got all of what they wanted, but they each got most of what they wanted. The result was that shift coverage had been addressed effectively. And it was decided that if someone left, the new hire would be asked to agree to the shift of the person they were replacing until a new schedule for the following six months was developed with their input.

The manager alone could never have figured out how to respond to the various needs of the team members, which included religious holidays, vacations, dependent care, personal events, and different capabilities. It took the entire team to include each other's needs, hear each other's voices, and come up with a winning solution for all. One result was a decrease in absenteeism, because people felt they had made a personal commitment to the group to be there when they said they would.

At Organization E, managers had historically been rewarded only for the accomplishment of tasks, with little focus on or concern about how they managed to achieve those results. Many managers were achieving satisfactory business results if one looked only at the surface. The full picture, however, revealed areas in which turnover was high or employee complaints were frequent.

Organization E realized that managers needed to be evaluated on multiple levels. While achieving results on one hand, they were also costing the organization money because many people were under performing and talented people were leaving the organization. Because of the lack of management skills and competencies, the human resources and employee relations departments spent most of their time addressing the concerns that people were raising due to the negative climate created by their managers.

The senior leaders at Organization E understood the need for change because of the effect these issues were having on the bottom line. In addition to committing to a significant change effort, the ability to coach, lead and motivate a diverse workforce was added to the performance scorecard of managers at all levels.

The leaders continued to make it clear that these new skills were not nice-to-haves but must haves. Although many perceived the change as just another add-on, senior leaders knew that if these competencies were not in place, they could not achieve their aggressive objectives or succeed in the future. Absence of these key performance-enhancing competencies would undermine many talented people in the organization, especially those who were not like the members of the traditional work group.

The goal was to redefine what it meant to be qualified. Many managers, who never expected to spend their time managing people or managing a diverse workforce, were required to learn a new definition of competence and change the ways they behaved and managed. Further, the new definition and need for new behaviors extended to everyone in the workforce. For some managers, the change was impossible; they had to be reassigned. For others, the new set of expectations was achievable, and these managers embarked on a journey of learning and development. It also created a breakthrough in what it meant to be a manager—promotion and succession lists changed and a new image began to take hold. Senior leaders also had to reinforce the understanding that the new criteria and new culture were permanent changes.

Next, the focus was to make managers not only accountable for completion of tasks but also for their ability to leverage the talent of their people. In addition to developing, respecting, and retaining people, they needed to demonstrate that they were supporting each individual in their ability to contribute more fully to the organization. Were they coaching and developing people? Were they providing honest feedback and evaluations? How did the people reporting to them experience the work environment? Did they feel included in matters affecting their work? Were they fairly treated? Were there fewer complaints? Were turnover and attrition reduced? Were performance problems addressed directly? Could the manager bring together a diverse team and support and nurture its efforts to achieve higher performance? Were there noticeable differences in the output of project teams and in each person's ability to contribute?

Organization E's senior leaders had to change the rules for success and evaluation. They could not give mixed signals about the new requirements, and had to stand fast in their commitment to raising these expectations and standards for success.

Many long-term managers questioned the new competency requirements and wondered whether they had to follow them or could just hold their collective breaths and let this program of the month pass. Many people were skeptical that the organization would actually adhere to these new competencies. But in time, and with determination and a sustained effort, the organization discovered and maximized the benefits of the new policies.

THE 11 INCLUSIVE BEHAVIORS

The key competencies for creating an Inclusion Breakthrough begin with 11 Inclusive Behaviors (Jensen, 1995). The behaviors cross industry lines, apply to start-up companies and nuclear power plants, not-for-profit organizations and dot-coms, government agencies, and Fortune 500 companies. People at all levels learn and demonstrate these behaviors. Acquiring, demonstrating, and rewarding these behaviors is absolutely necessary if an organization is to create a truly inclusive work culture.

These competencies move the organization and its individuals to a breakthrough in interactions and expectations. When combined, they lead to the inclusion of all people and their talents, as well as a new level of working together—teamwork that leads to innovation and creativity and establishes an environment that enables people to do their best work.

All individuals must learn to greet others authentically

From the moment people arrive at work, they must feel that they are part of the organizational community. All too often, people are in such a hurry to get to their e-mails or their voice mails that they miss the real people along the way. A simple hello and acknowledgment of others is a key first step to creating a more inclusive work environment.

One CEO took to heart the power of hellos. He was extremely introverted and avoided going to the cafeteria because he was afraid he would forget names and look foolish. However, he came to recognize how vital it was that people in the organization saw him and had direct contact with him. He learned that he did not need to know all about them; they were pleased just to get a greeting from him.

Another CEO required that people greet each other at every board meeting. When a meeting with outside investors went better than previous meetings, he credited this behavior with making the difference by opening the door to greater communication.

Individuals must create a sense of safety for themselves and their team members

All people must know that they will be accepted for who they are and for the perspectives, ideas, and skills they bring. The goal is to create an environment in which people feel psychologically and emotionally safe to share. If people feel constantly judged, if their ideas are repeatedly attacked or ignored, they will be reluctant to share their thinking and may withhold valuable ideas.

Part of the challenge is that safety means different things to different people. Creating safety does not mean creating an environment that is risk-averse. It means fostering an environment of respect for and acknowledgment of different people's needs and approaches. The starting point is to discuss what people need to feel safe and what can be done to build trust among individuals and team members.

In one education session, an African American woman explained that she was willing to stay late to deal with last-minute needs when she was in an organization in which she felt valued and acknowledged. In situations where she felt that going the extra mile was not valued or her effort seen, however, she was unwilling to work beyond what was required.

In another organization, a team described an organizational norm of teasing people publicly. For many people, this created an unsafe environment. No one gave feedback directly; instead, it came in the form of teasing humor, which many experienced as humiliation. After much discussion, people in the organization found ways to express humor without it being at an individual's expense and created a more trusting, safer environment in which to give respectful feedback.

In a truly inclusive environment misunderstandings are addressed and disagreements resolved as soon as possible
Misunderstandings and disagreements occur in every organization and in every relationship. All too often, people are shut down if they bring

a different approach to the table. Others try to ignore misunderstandings, hoping that the disagreement will just go away. In fact, teams cannot achieve their highest performance without raising differences in perspectives and having disagreements. These disagreements are needed to foster the creative tension that, when worked through, enables teams to break through barriers and exceed expectations.

The more that diversity is allowed to flourish, the more that conflicts and disagreements will arise as people share their varied perspectives and ideas. The challenge is to not suppress those disagreements and differences but rather to address them in ways that provide the opportunity for new thinking and ideas.

One approach that many organizations find useful is to create structures that legitimize putting any conflict or disagreement on the table. In one organization, staff meetings begin with public acknowledgments of jobs and actions performed well, and then continue with an opportunity for people to raise any conflicts or "pinches" (Glidewell & Sherwood, 1973) that may exist. This creates a legitimate structure in which to raise conflicts and misunderstandings.

Team members must take the time to listen, listen, listen, and respond when people share their ideas, thoughts, and perspectives
Team members must ask questions or restate a speaker's contribution until that individual feels understood. Being understood does not mean being in agreement—it simply means that each person knows she or he has been heard. Frequently, what happens instead is that people first share their differing perspectives and then argue with no resolution, or the group moves on as if what was said has no meaning. This results in people feeling alone and disconnected. It is critical that each individual feels heard and understood, and that the process overtly builds upon and responds to others' ideas, thoughts and perspectives. A key component of being heard is that others not only listen but also respond. In too many organizational cultures, the rule of silence prevails—individuals put their ideas out, no one

responds, and the group just continues on. A key to successful inclusion is to listen, listen, listen, and then respond.

Everyone must communicate clearly, directly, and honestly
Communicating clearly does not work unless the information is directed at the people who need to hear it and the message is candid and honest.

In most organizations, people have learned to guard their information. Instead of being candid and honest in their communications they attempt to be political. Few people want to be the bearers of bad news. Therefore, leaders and others often do not hear what is really going on in an organization. This can lead to decisions being made without full information—and these decisions are often doomed to fail. On an individual level, one of the biggest barriers in a work environment occurs when individuals do not get candid information about their performance. When there is an inclusion breakthrough, individuals are willing to speak their truths and share what they know candidly, so that decisions and actions are based on solid, valid information.

Everyone on the team needs to understand the group's tasks and how each task relates to the mission of the organization
Clarifying the vision at the outset is essential, but asking for re-clarification throughout the life of a project is valuable and productive as well. This will remind the team of the effect it is having, or needs to be having, on the organization's bottom line. It is essential that each individual and each team understand how their work provides value to the organization. One of the core tenets of an inclusive organization is to create an environment in which all people add value. Understanding how one's work supports the organization's direction and vision provides a valuable link to feeling that one performs meaningful work.

Every person on the team has a contribution to make, so make sure *all* voices are heard

Part of the job of creating a more inclusive environment is encouraging others to contribute and ensuring that the appropriate voices, whether in the room or not, are heard. It is helpful for a team to ask itself, "Have we heard from everyone?" "Who else needs to be included in this decision to make sure that all the issues have been addressed?" The core competence is to recognize that including all stakeholders at the front end saves time, money, and resources later on. And if people on the team are not seen as having contributions to make, the next question is, "Why are they here?"

Ask other team members to share their thoughts and experiences, and accept all frames of reference

If we truly believe that each person has a contribution to make, we need to find ways to understand each person's frame of reference based on her or his unique experiences and perspective. The team needs to understand that the sum of the whole is *always* greater than the sum of the individual parts. Each contribution sparks new thoughts and remembered experiences that can enhance the quality and success of a project's outcome.

Notice the behavior of each person on the team, and speak up if you think people are being excluded

Invite quiet members to speak and assure them that their contributions are essential. It takes a concerted effort to change behavior patterns. The assumption that people will speak up if they have something to say is incorrect. If the objective is to encourage new ideas and the richest and best thinking, all members of the team must be responsible for the team's efforts.

Make careful choices about when the team will meet and what it will work on

Be respectful of everyone's time. Each member must know that her or his participation is critical to the success of the team's work. In too many organizations, meetings are held without much consideration of an individual's personal needs. Does Harry have to pick up his children from day care at 4:30 P.M. every day? Does Sue have a parent-care situation that keeps her from arriving at the office before 9 A.M.? Being mindful of the needs of team members sends the signal that each person counts and each person's contribution is not only welcomed but necessary.

And finally, *be brave*

New behaviors involve taking risks. Be prepared to make some mistakes along the way. Don't assume that mistakes mean failure; rather, they are learning opportunities for the entire team. Accountabilities for learning and using new competencies and rewards must evolve as well. The most challenging task is to practice new ways of behaving, to resist following established norms, processes and procedures just *because*. To create an inclusive work culture that leverages diversity, each person must deal with the discomfort of change. To lean into learning new behaviors, people must have the courage to speak out, learn, grow, and work differently. As individuals they must break through their old behaviors, just as the organization is working to break through patterns and process at the systems level.

Organizational Capabilities and Individual Competencies

At Organization F, a long-established company, the challenge of global competition led to a serious re-examination of the competencies needed for success, not only in its new hires or managers but also across the entire organization. As an information-intensive organization with offices around the world, the organization's senior executives realized that they needed communication to flow freely, actively, and responsively throughout the organization's dispersed work groups. They also needed to be able to retain and recruit highly talented people from all parts of the world and tailor new products and services for customers in virtually every industry around the globe.

Organization F was a recent spin-off from its parent organization and realized that to succeed as a new company it needed a new culture. The spin-off was a signal to everyone that it was going to do business differently. More was going to be asked of people to meet marketplace demands. That meant overhauling all aspects of the business, including the ways in which people interacted, managed, and worked together. It was also an opportunity to reach levels of performance previously considered unattainable.

In identifying the skill sets and capabilities required to meet its competitive business needs, Organization F made a distinction between the organizational capabilities and the individual competencies it would require. The former included the kind of work environment and policy structure needed to support the organization's strategic objectives and direction. Individual competencies included what was required of each person to create and support the organizational capabilities.

For example, as part of its inclusion breakthrough strategy, Organization F's senior executives embarked on an education process to learn the requisite skills and become models for inclusive behaviors and practices. They communicated in their words and actions to everyone at Organization F the meaning behind the new behavioral requirements and how the new competencies were related to the organization's business objectives. The ability to provide this kind of meaning and direction was seen as a core leadership role, a mission critical leadership competency in itself.

Organization F identified and constructed organizational capabilities and individual competencies, to guide its actions and provide paths and strategies it could evaluate both short and long term.

Organization F identified its policies and practices as key tools in creating the necessary organizational capabilities for leveraging diversity and creating a culture of inclusion. Organization F's effort consisted of five organizational capabilities as shown in Table 1. Each capability built upon and supported the others.

To achieve the organizational capabilities, all associates, managers, and senior executives were expected to demonstrate the competencies listed in Table 2.

Organization F started with a road map for all associates, because these were the baseline skills expected of everyone. Then it created an additional layer for managers and an additional layer for senior executives, based on the recognition that each level of the organization holds greater responsibility for the effort and the culture.

Ensuring that individuals at all levels were acquiring the baseline individual competencies was only one step toward achieving an inclusion breakthrough.

Organizational capabilities would provide the institutional supports required to enable a higher-performing, inclusive work culture. Organization F was striving to transform itself in every dimension to be:

- **An employer of choice:** to retain, attract and develop talent

- **A business partner of choice:** to compete effectively in the marketplace

- **A stock of choice:** to attract investors

These enabling structures fostered more flexibility and the ability to respond faster to the changing marketplace. The need for leveraging diversity and building inclusion was integrated into day-to-day work strategies and practices. Performance reviews and individual development plans supported accountability at all levels. All members participated in skill-development activities. Organization-wide communication systems were kept at the leading edge of technological capability.

GAUGING THE RESULTS

As part of its ongoing process of enrolling and energizing people in learning and practicing the skills for leveraging diversity and building inclusion, Organization F's Diversity and Inclusion Action

Table 1: Organizational capabilities

TALENTED WORKFORCE TO MEET CURRENT AND PROJECTED NEEDS	PARTNERING FOR 360° VISION	COMMUNITY OF INCLUSION AND DIVERSITY	CULTURE OF RESPECT AND STRAIGHT TALK	STRUCTURES THAT FOSTER FLEXIBILITY AND CHOICE
• Key people retained and treated as valuable assets • Benchmark, identify, and communicate requisite skills and competencies for future needs • Recruitment and selection of new people is focused and highly successful • Employees, managers, and senior leaders demonstrate competencies and are held accountable for supporting the inclusion breakthrough	• Work teams provide 360-degree vision for problem solving and addressing customer needs and opportunities • Employees' ideas are utilized in problem solving • Shift from vendor to business partner relationship with customers • Partner effectively in and across units	• People have a feeling of belonging • A diverse workforce that mirrors company customers and the communities • Work/family/life flexibility and support • Community of inclusion and high performance at all company locations • The company is known in the communities where it has offices for being a preferred employer and preferred workplace	• People are clear and connected to organization goals and culture, co-workers and leaders • Leaders engage, inform, and enroll all people in inclusion breakthrough • Leaders encourage and reward risk taking • People are informed about items that affect their work • People experience being treated as individuals with respect and value • People are given the feedback they need to be successful	• Leveraging diversity and a culture of inclusion are integrated into day-to-day work structures and practice • Policies and practices support preferred employer, preferred workplace, and culture of inclusion • Performance evaluation processes support accountability at all levels

Table 2: Individual competencies

ALL ASSOCIATES	MANAGERS	SENIOR EXECUTIVES
• Teamwork: Partnering with others • Respect: Listening and responding to others • Addressing conflict: Leaning into discomfort • Straight Talk: Clear and direct communication • Belonging: Greeting and including people • Being brave: Encouraging change	**Associate competencies and** • Leading inclusive teams • Developing and retaining people • Coaching and mentoring others • Modeling and creating a culture of inclusion • Leveraging the diversity of all people	**Manager competencies and** • Connecting with all people • Integrating leveraging diversity and a culture of inclusion into business plans, strategies, and daily actions • Providing direction, focus, connections, and meaning to the inclusion breakthrough

Group interviewed managers, group leaders, and individual contributors throughout the organization, asking for descriptions of how things had changed. The group documented enough improvements in individual job satisfaction and organizational performance to justify continued investment in the culture change effort.

An excerpt from the
Organization F company newsletter:

What has changed since the Leveraging Diversity and Inclusion effort started?

Overall Associates:
More people are challenging each other about their behavior.

People are more informed and better connected to the strategies and direction of the organization.

There are more partnerships across lines of business and geographies.

People express positive feelings about the organization's move to being market-driven.

The local Chamber of Commerce and the Hispanic Business Association recognized the organization as a Preferred Employer for its efforts and diversity.

All people believe there are more opportunities inside the organization.

The Gay-Lesbian-Bisexual-Transgender Alliance has over 60 members as part of the network.

People believe that the organization is serious about the inclusion initiative.

Managers:
Managers are beginning to practice inclusive behaviors.

Managers are putting inclusion on the agenda in their staff meetings.

When the effort began, it was not unusual for people to be fearful of raising issues with their managers and to follow a strict protocol. People are more willing today to raise issues concerning the organization to their managers and with their peers.

After a Manager Education Session, a manager initiated a luncheon every other month for managers at their sites. It is a cross-functional group. These managers had never before gotten together. They are now working on solving business problems together.

Senior Executives:

Senior executives are more known by associates than in the past, and people feel more positive about them.

People see the senior executives as more focused and aligned.

Senior executives are taking responsibility for engaging and enrolling all members of the organization in the Inclusion Breakthrough.

The payoff for Organization F was a higher standard of expertise— the capability to leverage greater talent—as expressed in the following quotes from leaders:

> "Communications have improved greatly from
> the top down. People see that it starts right at the top. ...
> The newsletter has been a positive vehicle. You really get
> the impact when it is a monthly communication from the
> president or the chairman of the board."

And from associates:

> "People are openly talking about differences of
> ethnic groups and behaviors for inclusion. I see more of
> the white members leaning into that and feeling
> more comfortable with it."

"There had been a history of (initiatives being like) a flavor of the month. But people see this as something that's not going away. People are wanting to get more involved."

"I'm very surprised to see something on this every month in the newsletter. And every two or three months they are doing a big insert or foldout, including volunteerism— that's a very big thing. It's showing that the inclusion and diversity effort is not just about bringing in minorities. There is volunteerism, mentoring, networks and some other things. And it is just the beginning."

"There is a new thing as far as sales is concerned in terms of the way we do business. We are paying more attention to the way we deliver information to all our customers."

"The biggest thing that has happened has been the big, big impact on people of color. They see there is some room and opportunity for advancement where before they didn't see any. Obviously, you have to have the skills, but now there is room."

"Members from different backgrounds have different concerns. The Gay and Lesbian Network has really taken off. The African American Network has really taken off. So have the Hispanic Network, Asian American Network and the Women's Network, and a wellness group for people with disabilities. The more we can get those support groups going ... that's very positive."

"People are saying hello to one another. We are
creating a sense of community."

"In making project assignments we are now very aware
of inclusion as a criterion and the importance of a
diverse makeup of the team."

"Morale has improved throughout the organization."

Creating a new set of competencies and new expectations is only
one step in creating an inclusion breakthrough. For such an effort to
be sustained, every system, policy, and process must support the new
competencies.

Enabling Policies and Practices

No matter how stringently an organization *requires* people to learn new sets of competencies and behaviors, no significant or sustainable change will occur unless the organization's established rules, written and unwritten, change also.

What gets measured, monitored, and rewarded is what matters. It follows, then, that new competencies must be integrated into performance reviews, evaluations, developmental plans, merit rewards, and recognition programs. In the absence of these enabling and accountability mechanisms, people will not have any tangible reason to change or consequences for their noncompliance or defiance. Unless the inclusion breakthrough is integrated into the organization's policies and practices, the new required competencies will be relegated to a wish list.

Organization G was hit with a class-action suit, charging the organization with systematic performance appraisal and career-pathing bias against people of color and white women. An independent study of performance appraisals and promotion records showed that people of color and white women consistently received lower performance ratings than those received by white men, particularly when the managers conducting the appraisals were white men. Even when performance appraisals were similar across gender

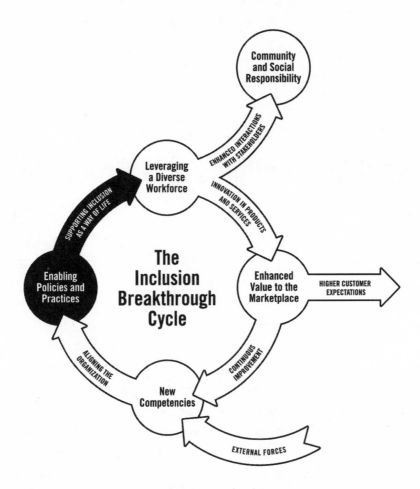

and racial lines, people of color and white women were not promoted as rapidly as their white male counterparts. Interviews with managers revealed that many gave higher scores to people with whom they had personal relationships, socialized more often, and were more comfortable.

Although there were few allegations of overt racism or sexism, the damage from these comfort-based appraisals was tangible enough for Organization G to agree to a multi-million-dollar settlement. Although the cost of the settlement was substantial, the incalculable cost of the problem—decades of preventing many people from giving their best efforts and a workforce in upheaval—was even greater.

To sustain an inclusion breakthrough and create the desired new culture, it is essential that all aspects of the organization's policies and practices be aligned with the new set of competencies. Without such alignment, it is hard to unleash the real power of diversity. These policies and practices must support the aspired-to culture and connect the inclusion breakthrough to the mission, vision, and values of the organization.

A HARD LOOK AT SOFT POLICIES

As is true of most issues that have direct dollars-and-cents implications, compensation is usually considered to be a core business issue—a hard item, as opposed to soft items such as personal-leave policies, health-care benefits, in-service training programs, and after-hours recreation programs.

But compensation is one of the least important factors in creating a culture of inclusion that can help retain and attract a highly talented group of people. As long as compensation is perceived as fair and in the general vicinity of the industry average, it becomes a nonissue. What inspires individuals to invest their energies and passions, and what inspires work teams to leverage their disparate talents are the soft policies and practices—the ones that help connect people to their workplace and to each other and support their life.

If the workplace is hostile or unsupportive, if it doesn't evoke a sense of connection, respect, and belonging, if there is no possibility for growth, development, or meaningful work, no amount of money will keep talented people there for long. In fact, since the demise of the job-for-life concept, many people hold the workplace to a higher standard and want more intangibles that offer them day-to-day support. Prime among them is a physical and behavioral infrastructure that enables people to participate as individuals, including all their differences, while allowing them to connect with one another and work effectively in partnerships and teams.

OUTMODED POLICIES AND PRACTICES

The typical organization's policies and practices can be a mind-boggling maze of job descriptions, management philosophies, leadership styles, and unspoken understandings, with each business unit having its own strategy, its own culture, even its own language. The potential for misunderstandings, internal competition and duplicated or counter-productive efforts is huge.

One necessary change is to throw out old assumptions. Traditional organizational policies and practices were based on a host of outmoded assumptions, including the following:

- People came into the organization at the bottom, underwent a hazing period, and worked their way up.

- The road to success looked like a bus route with many required stops. If you sat in the right seat for the right length of time you would get to your destination.

- You hired people that you were familiar with in some way—school colleagues and even family and friends—people with whom you felt comfortable.

- Results meant hitting your numbers, with the how not mattering much.

- Top positions merited top perks: preferred parking spaces, executive dining room access, first call for overtime and bonuses.

- Following the chain of command—communication only between direct reports and no skipping levels—was the most effective way to accomplish things.

- The company had a Christmas party—"everyone's" holiday—and observed holidays when everyone got paid time off: Thanksgiving, New Year's Day, Easter. People who practiced a "different" religion had to ask permission to take their religious holidays as personal days and were often required to find someone to cover for them.

ENACTING CHANGES IN POLICY

Some organizations pore over best practices reports and then invest heavily in programs that have worked well in other organizations. Without a connection to the mission, strategies of the organization, and an integrated plan to achieve an inclusion breakthrough, the best practices of one organization may translate to nothing more than the flavor-of-the-month program for another.

One analogy for thinking about organizational policies as infrastructure is the difference between a skyscraper and a campsite. Skyscrapers are built to meet a need as defined by the time they are designed. When they are completed, those needs have often shifted, rendering the structure outdated. A campsite, on the other hand, is built to respond to what is needed today. It is easy to tear down, move, modify, or abandon if rapid changes in direction occur tomorrow.

When it comes to policies and practices to support an inclusion breakthrough, organizations need campsites, not skyscrapers. External changes come rapidly today, and organizations are scrambling to keep up. They—and their policies—must adapt even more rapidly in the future.

Following are some of the updated policies and practices that can significantly boost retention, recruitment, and the development of a diverse and productive talent pool. Some are becoming commonplace; others may seem a stretch and require an organization to re-evaluate its policies.

HIRING

More and more organizations are treating prospective hires as core assets, finding ways to acknowledge them and make them feel valued even before hiring them.

While it is not unusual for organizations to lavish great expense and attention on prized recruits, it is less common for them to pay the same amount of attention to their retention and development after they are hired. Some organizations are inviting all candidates to interview a diverse group of people so that the candidates can learn the truth about the organization before they join. Others assign newly hired people a buddy, which takes the traditional orientation beyond the usual walkthrough or half-day training session: "Here's your desk, here's the bathroom, good luck." The buddy is responsible for making the new person feel part of the organization and getting the new person up to speed. Practices like these recognize that a person's degree of integration into the community of the organization early on has a great effect on her or his ultimate success there.

It is even more important for people who are not like the organization's traditional group to have support mechanisms available—individuals who can help reduce isolation and address policies, practices and people that might be barriers to their success.

At Organization H, a multinational corporation with locations in many countries, a newly hired Latino was asked to move far from his extended family. A critical factor in his decision to accept the new position was the way his new colleagues extended themselves to him. They invited him and his immediate family to their homes and introduced him to people inside and outside the organization who might have similar interests. They followed his lead and acknowledged his cultural identity to the degree that he wanted it acknowledged and learned about which holidays he celebrated. They treated him like he had been there as long as they had been there without any new person hazing or isolation. The personal impact of separation from one's extended family is different across cultures. Few people like to be uprooted, but for people who are deeply connected to their broader families, the personal and emotional cost of such a move increases considerably. The organization's willingness to support him inside and outside of work not only helped influence his decision but also helped him to succeed.

Performance appraisal systems

Performance review processes are one of the most influential practices in an organization. Recognizing that reviews are often sources of bias, some organizations have decided to throw them out altogether. Others have transformed the performance review system into a process of quarterly development discussions, recognizing that people need to continually learn and grow so that they stay marketable. Some organizations scan the patterns of performance appraisals for covert biases that may be negatively affecting specific groups.

Rewards and scorecards

Organizations committed to an inclusion breakthrough know they must develop scorecards and measurement systems that integrate personal development, coaching, and retention with organizational results. In some organizations, the senior leaders' incentive compensation is directly related to their ability to model and lead an inclusion breakthrough.

Organization I, a technology company, saw people as core assets critical to organizational success. In the performance assessments of the organization's managers and leaders, one of the five key objectives for evaluation focused on the development of their direct reports. If a new hire was unsuccessful, it was considered the responsibility of the manager *and* the individual. In this way, managers had more at stake in the game to ensure the success of the people they brought in.

Employee networks

Network groups (sometimes called affinity groups) may be established where people come together for mutual support and to add value to the organization by utilizing the increased acceptance and inclusion of one social identity group. These groups are actually business partnerships assisting in the success of the organization through mentoring and developing their members, as well as outreach to customers and potential new hires.

Often these groups are initially formed solely for members of a specific social identity group to find a place of support and to learn how to succeed in the organization. Over time, many of them include a focus on the business opportunities present in the marketplace and opportunities to leverage individuals' talents in the organization. In some organizations today, individuals of a specific social identity group and their allies join together to address these challenges and opportunities.

Examples of such network groups include people in the organization with disabilities, single parents, people of a specific racial identity, or a network of people of color or women. Community and customer outreach to that specific social identity group is often included as part of their objectives, in addition to supporting and mentoring each other and helping others understand the opportunities that specific social identity groups offer to the organization. The outreach includes recruiting new people who might be members of that social identity group and identifying business opportunities.

Some organizations with the most successful networks have maintained open memberships. A women's network, for example, will include men who are committed to supporting women in the organization; lesbian, gay, and bisexual groups include heterosexuals committed to opportunities and concerns related to those groups.

Benefits packages

Many organizations are changing their benefits packages to support a more inclusive work culture and meet the needs of different populations by offering a variety of benefits, such as preventative health care.

To retain and recruit people, businesses such as Fannie Mae, Harley-Davidson and Xerox offer employees housing assistance in the form of forgivable or low-interest loans, rental subsidies, or grants to cover closing costs. A recent survey of 600 workforce administrators showed that 6 percent of employers offer mortgage and rental assistance to employees, and an additional 3 percent offer cash toward a down payment. Yale University, Howard University, and Russell Sage College bought and restored housing in distressed neighborhoods near their campuses and created financial incentives for their people to purchase these homes. Soaring real estate prices prompted the San Francisco Unified School District to build a 43-unit apartment complex for teachers and the Santa Clara, California Unified School District to offer housing grants for its teachers (Los Angeles Times, Jan. 28, 2001).

Domestic partner benefits

Although still controversial in some places, domestic partner benefits must be offered if organizations don't want to exclude a significant talent pool and current or future customer base. To create an inclusion breakthrough, organizations need to do more than offer baseline benefits—they must offer the benefits that provide opportunities for partners as they do for married couples.

Extended parental leave

The standard two- or three-month parental leave is not nearly enough. Organizations wanting to retain top talent cannot afford to let people walk out the door over limited parental leave policies. That is why some companies are offering such options as one-year maternity or paternity leave, two years of part-time work assignments, flextime or job-sharing. Some also extend eligibility for those benefits to all relevant social identity groups such as mothers, fathers, lesbians, gays, and adoptive parents.

Floating holidays

Flexible days off allow each person to define which days are holidays, instead of basing them on the preferences of the founding members or the dominant group.

Flexible work schedules

Flextime offers many people the opportunity and the means to stay with an organization, allowing them to work during the hours when they can do their most productive work.

THE NEW BASELINE

It is critical to pay attention and ensure that *all* policies and practices enable all people in the organization to operate and perform at a new level of contribution. In addition, for an inclusion breakthrough, organizations must go beyond baseline actions and raise the bar on how their policies and practices support individuals from a wide range of social identity groups.

Addressing issues relating to people of color

Many organizations undertake proactive retention and recruitment efforts aimed at people of color. Baseline activities may include retaining diversity recruiters, implementing community outreach programs, and establishing networks to increase support for and representation of people of color. These efforts often yield increased representation and create a more diverse pipeline that over time is expected to affect the numbers of women of color and men of color at all levels of the organization.

Other organizations understand that one cannot lump all people of color together. For example, a demographic analysis may reveal scant representation of Asian Americans or Latinos and Latinas at any level of the organization, while African Americans may be represented only at entry level and some managerial levels. Recognizing this differentiation between groups translates into targeted recruitment efforts.

Baseline:

- Proactive retention and recruitment efforts

- Some representation at all levels
- Addressing differentiation between groups

The new baseline demands not only representation throughout the organization but a critical mass at all levels. This ensures that people are not isolated, that there truly is a viable pipeline and not a case of "We had one once but she left and we can't find any more." It guarantees that people of color have multiple role models and peers, and that each person of color can be seen as a differentiated individual, not as a full-time representative of her or his group.

As a critical mass is achieved, it is necessary to understand that many people do not consider themselves solely Asian American or African American but rather of multiracial identity. These individuals need to be heard and seen as unique individuals and as a unique social identity group. The new baseline also calls for two-way mentoring across racial lines. This enables individuals to learn from one another, with the goal being of developing understanding and skills for partnering across lines of difference, not learning how to fit into the old culture. Similarly, support networks are created not as a way to help people assimilate, but as a vital career development, inclusion and organizational success mechanism.

The new baseline:

- Critical mass at all levels
- Inclusion of people of multiracial identity
- Two-way mentoring and support networks

Addressing issues relating to lesbians, gays and bisexuals

There is new and growing recognition of the importance of addressing the needs of individuals who are lesbian, gay, bisexual, or transgendered. Some organizations have found it difficult to address this issue because they define it as a moral question, rather than understanding it as the productivity issue and opportunity it truly represents. For many service and consumer-product organizations, it is also a customer issue and opportunity.

For organizations working toward achieving a more diverse and inclusive workplace, the first priority must be creating a safe place for lesbians and gays to come out in the organization. It must be made clear that this is a business imperative. Far too many people who are lesbian or gay experience hostile work environments in which jokes and biased remarks are allowed to prevail, and divulging one's sexual orientation would negatively affect her or his career opportunities.

A baseline practice supporting people who are lesbian or gay is guaranteed access to the same organizational benefits granted people who are heterosexual. At a fundamental level, this means offering domestic partner benefits. Taking this step without creating a safe place, however, keeps many lesbian and gay people from feeling comfortable enough to take advantage of the benefits being offered.

Baseline:

- A Safe Place^{TM}

- Domestic partner benefits

Organizations committed to an inclusion breakthrough must do much more than create a safe place and offer benefits. They must see all people as team members and be willing to create an environment that is welcoming and inclusive of all. This means making sure that people's partners are welcomed at company functions, including being able to dance together if others are dancing. It means creating an environment in which lesbian and gay people can talk openly with colleagues about the sickness or death of a partner or about their weddings and breakups. And organizations that provide perks to peoples' family members need to extend that definition to include partners of people who are lesbian or gay. At one university, for example, people at certain levels are given tuition reimbursement for their spouses. Lesbian and gay couples are not given the same benefit.

The new baseline also means recognizing that customers may be lesbian or gay and that the development of inclusive products, services and advertising to meet their needs represents a genuine opportunity.

The new baseline:

- Partners welcomed at company functions

- Incorporating lesbian and gay cultures into organizational events

- Medical coverage that takes into account the unique needs of lesbian, gay, bisexual, and transgendered people

- Inclusion in advertising and product development, and focusing advertising in the lesbian and gay communities

Addressing issues relating to women

For decades, women in the workplace have faced the challenges of not being treated as full partners. Preventing sexual harassment and supporting work, life, and family integration are part of the baseline for the full integration of women today. In some organizations, the effort to achieve greater inclusion for women is beginning to pay off, with a critical mass of women present at all levels of the organization.

The baseline of such efforts includes smashing the glass ceiling—barriers that limit women from reaching the top—and moving women out of staff functions into line jobs, interfacing with customers or the production and delivery of services, so that they can assume every position of power and leadership. Some organizations are working not only to enable women to contribute, but also to degender roles and positions by going beyond just having women on the payroll. That means upgrading the types of positions women occupy and the value they can deliver, as well as valuing the work that women do in the organization at all levels and functions. The de-gendering of the workplace opens more avenues for success and acknowledges that leaders can embody many different approaches and styles.

Baseline:
- Critical mass at all levels
- Addressing the glass ceiling
- Degendering roles and positions

Although many organizations have done a good job of developing formal policies and practices to address overt sexual harassment, the new baseline seeks to identify and eliminate the more subtle forms of harassment. It focuses not only on what *not* to do, but also on creating a new set of inclusive behaviors that enable women and men to partner effectively across genders. The new baseline also goes beyond the glass ceiling and begins to address the sticky floor—barriers that keep women of color and other women stuck at lower levels. The new baseline does not lump all women together but addresses the distinct challenges faced by white women and women of color (and the differentiation among women of color), and the different experiences and needs of women who are in staff, managerial, and individual contributor roles.

The new baseline recognizes that in the past, flextime applied only to women in professional positions, telecommuting support was not extended to all, and individuals who participated in job-sharing or who took maternity leave made an implicit deal to be derailed from the career track. An inclusion breakthrough develops creative ways to support contributions in many different forms, recognizing the need for flexibility and negotiation of individual needs. The new baseline also recognizes the way in which work, life, and family issues have historically been associated with women and not men. Men with children also give more when their needs for work, life, and family integration are heard and considered.

The new baseline:

- Eliminating subtle harassment

- Two-way mentoring

- Addressing differentiation between women of color and white women

- Flextime applied to all positions, not just for exempt employees

- Women who job-share or take maternity leave continue to have career advancement opportunities

Addressing issues relating to white men

In many organizational frameworks of diversity and inclusion, white men are left out of the picture. It is assumed that because many white men have historically been successful, the organization already works for them and their needs do not need to be addressed. Some white men's resistance to diversity efforts arise from the fear that they are being excluded and diversity does not mean them. "White men need not apply" is evoked for many who read, "The organization is looking for a diverse candidate."

The baseline today is to ensure that white men are included in the organization's leveraging diversity and inclusion efforts. It creates an environment in which more than one type of white man can succeed and enhances white men's competencies to effectively partner, engage, manage, and interact in a more and more diverse organization.

Baseline:

- Enhanced competencies for leveraging diversity and building inclusion
- An environment in which more than one type of white man can succeed

The new baseline recognizes that white men need support on this journey. The new baseline creates safety for white men so they need not feel that they are the only source of the problems, and are enabled to develop the skills and abilities to integrate diversity, inclusion, and higher performance by being partners in the change process.

Strategies to achieve this goal include expanding networks to include white men in each network group and establishing two-way mentoring so that white men can explore their own diversity. Because white men are often in the one-up group, people don't think white men have anything to learn. However, the contrary is true. Many white men have been trapped in the traditional way of doing things as well, often blinded by their privilege. An open and honest two-way mentoring partnership gives white men a chance to learn about and see the organization and the world from another perspective. It also gives him the opportunity to receive coaching about how to better integrate diversity and inclusion into his work interactions and activities from someone he trusts.

The new baseline:

- Expand networks and two-way mentoring so that white men can explore their own diversity and how to be effective partners in the change process
- Recognize the work, life, and family integration issues of men

Addressing issues relating to nationality

Organizations are beginning to deal with the reality that they now encompass people and customers of many nationalities and cultural backgrounds. To be effective, the organization must be able to speak to all of its customers and clientele in their own languages. Some United States-based organizations have begun to pay a premium for individuals who speak languages other than English, recognizing that these skills are not just nice to have but also critical for organizational success. The baseline is to compensate individuals who have job-enhancing language skills with additional pay. For global organizations, the baseline is a recognition that their boards of directors must consist of at least more than one nationality.

Baseline:

- Additional pay for job-enhancing language skills
- Hiring, training and retention of people from a variety of continents

The new baseline challenges organizations to become truly multicultural. Reflecting that challenge, new practices must support a wide range of religious observances, holidays, dress, and customs, responding to different needs with respect to communication style, food, and language. Policies, practices and competencies to bring such a group together, whether in one locale or virtually, have become the new standard necessary for organizations.

Although many organizations describe themselves as global, few are reaching the new standard of what it means to be a global organization. The new baseline means leading and managing on a global basis: constituting leadership and a board of directors that represents the entire organization and all of its geographic locations, creating a corporate culture that speaks to all members of the organization, and instituting global management of the organization. That ensures that talent searches are global and local talent is developed, allowing local nationals to run local organizations and bring their voices, perspectives, and leadership to the corporate table.

The new baseline:

- Local nationals run local organizations
- Global leaders run global organizations

Addressing issues relating to organizational hierarchy

One of the greatest challenges facing organizations today is the issue of hierarchy. Most efforts to deal with it focus on ensuring that all people at all levels of the organization are treated with respect. This baseline understanding recognizes that to treat staff and administrative people as one-down or devalued does not support the inclusion and contributions of all people or the success of the enterprise. Programs are designed to develop the skills and attend to the career needs of people at all levels of the organization. The baseline shifts from the belief that a person's worth is based on her or his position to one that recognizes that worth is based on contribution.

Baseline:

- Individuals at all levels treated as essential and with respect
- Career and skill development available to people at all levels

The new baseline recognizes that each person needs to be the COO (Chief Operating Officer) of her or his job, and that all people can assume leadership and contribute to the organization's success. Staff members who have supported the work of the team are recognized and rewarded to convey the value the organization places on the contributions of all members.

As organizations flatten and recognize that talent exists at all levels, many old practices will change. The new baseline involves creating processes to engage individuals at all levels and hear all voices, especially individuals whose work will be affected by a decision or have key data to contribute to the process. The new baseline moves beyond traditional notions of staff meetings as including only direct reports. It opens meetings so that the right people are in the room to have the right conversation. Who needs to be at this meeting? Who is affected by what is decided? Who has the information? Often it is not the direct report but someone closer to the work project. Such skip level interventions signal that it is not rank but knowledge contribution and effect that matter.

The new baseline:

- Extended-level staff meetings

- Involvement of people at all levels in decision-making processes

Addressing issues relating to people with disabilities

People with disabilities are invisible in many organizations. People in wheelchairs are often kept isolated from their peers. People with less visible disabilities often hide their disabilities for fear of social ostracism or career-limiting consequences. It is generally assumed that people with physical disabilities have something wrong with them. And yet, this is one social identity group to which most of us, if we live long enough, will eventually belong. Considering this inevitability, it is surprising that the current baseline is so low.

In many ways, despite the Americans with Disabilities Act (ADA), most organizations have not lived up to the letter, or the spirit, of the law. For many, it seems easier and more cost-effective to build ramps and provide other access-compliant accommodations only when forced to by a threatening lawsuit or the glare of the public-opinion spotlight. With cuts in benefits, many organizations do not provide medical benefits that cover pre-existing conditions. When questioned about the inclusion or contributions of people with disabilities, many organization members reply, "I don't have any prejudice against them, but I don't think we have anybody like that."

The baseline today requires organizations to see people with disabilities as bringing value and potential to the organization. It is crucial to not pigeonhole people with disabilities into dead-end jobs or to assume what effect their impairments might have on their performance.

Baseline:

- Adhering to Americans with Disabilities Act legal requirements and assuring necessary accommodations are in place

- Providing medical/health benefits that address individual's needs

- Acknowledging people with disabilities have a place in the organization and contribute to its success

The new baseline creates a welcoming workplace for people with all kinds of disabilities. If physical barriers exist, few people with disabilities will want to spend their energy dealing with them—especially if more welcoming accommodations can be found elsewhere.

Retaining people with disabilities requires creating an environment in which it is safe for people to come forward with their needs and seek accommodations without negatively impairing their careers.

The new baseline:

- Proactive recruitment of and marketing to people with disabilities; inclusion in "high-potential" promotion lists, representation in advertising images

- Support networks and referral services for people with disabilities and their families

- Off-budget funding for productivity-enhancing support equipment and accommodations

Addressing issues relating to age

In many organizations, people around the age of 45 are considered old. People over 50 look for ways to conceal their age, wondering whether they will be next to receive a severance package just before they are eligible to retire. The baseline for organizations today is to address both sides of this equation: the need to recruit young people for the added value of youth while not casting out people who are 50 and older because of their age, thereby losing their accumulated wisdom and experience.

Baseline:

- Recruiting young people for the added value of youth

- Not casting out people 50 and older because of their age

The new baseline for an inclusion breakthrough means not only bringing in young people, but moving them up as quickly as possible. The need to find meaningful and challenging work for young people has become a requisite in organizations that understand the need to embrace everyone's contributions. They recognize that talented young people see the limitations in the pay for performance practice. Instead, young people see themselves as investments in the future of the organization and require pay for expectations. The new baseline recognizes and pays for potential talent with the expectation that salary and compensation can be adjusted if performance does not follow. "Pay me now and let me deliver" is the new baseline for many organizations seeking talented young people.

On the other side of the equation, the new baseline means extending the retirement age and finding creative ways to retain and engage the talents of older contributors, including 50-and-over people in high-potential groups and recognizing that age is a poor predictor of potential. In fact, studies show lower absenteeism and longer tenure expectations with people over the age of 50.

The new baseline:
- Move young people up as quickly as possible
- "Pay for expectations"
- Extend retirement age
- Include 50-and-over people in "high potential" groups

FAIRNESS AND BENEFITS

Critical to the new baseline is a redefinition of fairness. In many organizations, access to benefits is at the discretion of one's manager, which brings into play a host of inconsistencies based on individual biases or organizational conflicts. More and more organizations recognize that being fair means not treating everyone the same but creating an environment in which everyone gets what they need to do their best work.

In a city government's culture change effort, one of the primary goals was to provide equitable service to people in different communities, not equal service or the same service. This required an in-depth understanding of the realities and different needs of each area, each neighborhood, and each cultural group. It also required empowering the city employees to customize the services they offered to fit the needs of the people they served and holding them accountable for doing so.

The advantages of implementing new policies and practices are measured in terms of improved talent recruitment, development, and retention, increased productivity, reduced absenteeism, reduced incidence of lawsuits, and lower costs because people are working collaboratively, which reduces the waste of time and dollars. Significant but less measurable gains are evident in broader participation in decision-making processes, improved teamwork and team spirit, higher energy levels, greater levels of innovation, enhanced customer service, and greater feelings of connection to the organization and its mission. The outcome is a win-win situation for the organization, its individuals, its business partners, and its community.

Leveraging a Diverse Workforce

Most organizations believe that having a diverse workforce in itself will create value. In reality, having a diverse workforce is just having an under-leveraged asset unless there is strategic intent to unleash that diversity with the critical elements to support it. Less than that results in nothing more than a diversity in a box effort.

Strategies that focus on minimizing conflicts and other possible negative consequences of bringing different kinds of people together—are nothing more than status-quo strategies that maintain diversity in a box. To leverage diversity—to yield greater engagement, interaction, stimulation, and exploration of a wider range of possible solutions—disagreements and conflicts must be addressed.

Leveraging diversity means that differences are not ignored. When diversity is leveraged, innovation and creativity take hold from the sharing of new and different ideas, from the ability to create a new synthesis emerging from diverging points of views.

Organizations need people who are willing to bring new and different perspectives and skills. Perhaps even more, they need their current people to be willing and able to act in new and different ways. In a society that has made life difficult and dangerous for people who are new or different, this continues to be a major challenge for many United States-based individuals and organizations. As the

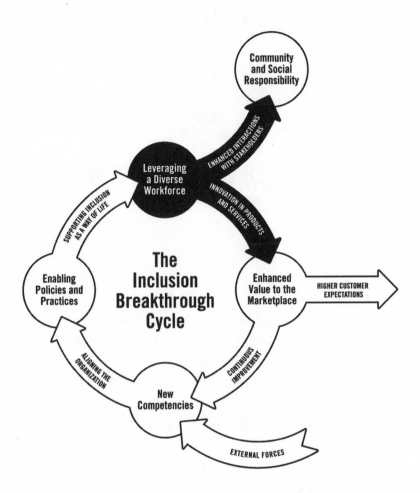

workforce becomes more diverse, the response from most organizations is to try to manage diversity, to contain it and keep it in a box. When people are forced to assimilate or keep their differences private and hidden, fitting in becomes their primary task. Just as important as building on what they have in common, creating workplaces that enable people to voice and build upon their differences is also essential. However, this is not an easy task.

THE *ISMS* ARE STILL WITH US

An inclusion breakthrough strives to unleash the power and potential of leveraging diversity. However, before an organization can hope to benefit from an inclusion breakthrough, it must address some significant barriers to inclusion. These barriers are embedded not just in organizational policies and practices but also in our societal and individual belief systems. They stem from the power and effect of *isms* in our society, our history, and our daily lives.

Historically, United States societal and organizational systems and culture have worked against people who are different from the traditional, dominant group. Unfortunately, this problem continues today.

Many people believe that diversity should be about tolerance—appreciating individual differences, not addressing the wrongs visited upon various social identity groups. Well-meaning or not, this stance keeps the dialogue and focus away from uncomfortable areas of power, privilege, and personal responsibility. It seeks to wash away the real barriers that separate us and tries to create a level playing field where none exists. Before any substantive change can take place in an organization, the people must understand that inequalities and injustices are a very real part of the everyday experiences of some and perhaps many of their team members.

Sexism, heterosexism, nationalism, classism, ableism and racism are a few expressions of the oppression that sits like a boulder on the unlevel playing field of most societies (see Figure 5). The same is true of most organizations. To support oppression and discrimination, all a person, group, or institution need do is take no action.

To keep the isms alive and powerful—to keep the dominance of the one-up group alive, to convince some that the one-down group deserves its plight, to keep "us" feeling threatened by "them"—all that is needed is a comment here and an inaction there, for example:

"Don't take it personally. You have to admit it's a funny joke."

"We all have to overcome some adversity in life."

"Have some patience. Look how far you people have come."

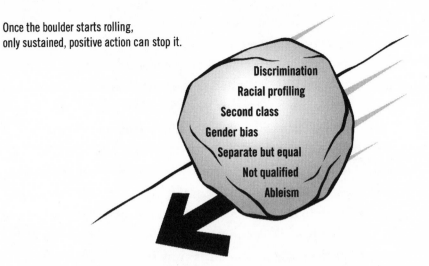

Once the boulder starts rolling,
only sustained, positive action can stop it.

Discrimination
Racial profiling
Second class
Gender bias
Separate but equal
Not qualified
Ableism

Figure 5. The boulder of oppression

"You're not like the rest of them. I don't think
of you as one of them."

"You can't fire them or give honest feedback
because you might get sued."

"You have to be careful around them or
you'll be accused of harassment."

"There is no budget for special accommodations
for people with disabilities."

"Women with children are distracted from their careers."

Daily newspaper headlines make it clear that, even with some
anti-discrimination legislation in place for years in the United States
and other countries, in many institutions discrimination continues—
sometimes subtle, sometimes blatant, sometimes inadvertent, sometimes coldly calculated. For example, in most places, lesbians and
gays can be legally dismissed from their jobs because of their sexual
orientation. In many organizations, single mothers receive fewer
promotions and salary increases than single women without children;

both groups lag behind single men. Women of color make substantially less than white women. People in wheelchairs or with other visible disabilities are absent from most organizations.

To achieve an inclusion breakthrough, one cannot go straight to inclusion. First, the boulder of bias and oppression must be removed, as must the self-fulfilling expectation that difference is a deficit.

Often, even people from the traditionally one-up group who have divergent ideas and operating styles do not feel free to express themselves lest they face the kind of discrimination they see being leveled against those who are one-down. The cost is high; mergers and partnerships fail to mesh, teamwork suffers, innovation is thwarted, tension builds, and energy is misdirected. Overall organizational performance significantly suffers.

Most organizations pride themselves on being fair. They want to believe that promotions are awarded based on merit. People at all levels strive to become color or gender blind—but that very blindness limits their ability to see the insidiousness of the barriers that exist.

For example:

- White women may express concern about their organization's glass ceiling, while remaining oblivious to the plight of women of color who are stuck to its sticky floor.

- Heterosexual people may enjoy generous benefit packages that cover their spouses and family members, without realizing that these same benefits are denied to their lesbian and gay colleagues.

- Men may be supported and admired by their colleagues when they need to leave work early to coach their child's soccer team, but women are judged negatively when they need to pick up their children at day care.

- A new white hire is seen as competent, but a new hire of color is assumed to be a less-qualified, Affirmative Action hire, regardless of her or his competence and past achievements.

Given the indisputable inequities in today's society, it is not surprising that the composition of most senior executive teams belies the notion of every person having an equal shot at climbing the organizational ladder. Not only is the playing field tilted against some groups, but many of society's basic institutions are also supporting the tilt. Racial profiling is an increasingly acknowledged practice. African Americans and Latinos still experience a significantly higher incidence of mortgage loan rejections than whites. When buying cars, Latinos and African Americans are often asked to make down payments 50 percent to 100 percent higher than whites.

The larger social context in which organizations exist makes it difficult to level the playing field inside organizations, yet organizations must overcome these difficulties if their workforce is going to do its best work. But leveling the playing field to where many in the dominant group are located is not good enough. Why settle for equal disadvantage? The goal should not be merely to level one end, but to raise the entire playing field so that everyone is supported to excel.

On a practical note, to achieve buy-in from the traditional group, an organizational culture change must clearly benefit them as well. Everyone—not just members of the identified target groups—must benefit. Charges of reverse discrimination may be labeled as resistance or an expression of sour grapes or even a heels-in-the-dirt attempt to maintain privilege. In fact, they are always an indication that those making the accusations feel left out, not included.

Organization J, a large manufacturing organization, was building a start-up plant and had worked hard to make it a state-of-the-art facility. The organization went through an extensive hiring process at all levels of the organization to bring in a highly diverse workforce from the local area.

The leaders were proud of their organization's diversity. Even before the plant opened, they had committed themselves to a team environment and had provided extensive training and education to all members of the workforce about working together effectively—

decision-making, team processes, listening skills, and dealing with conflicts. But over time the productivity of these diverse teams declined, and incidents of racism and sexism began to surface. Decisions were beginning to be made along racial and gender lines. Teams that were weighted with one group over another began to bring in people more like the majority, and teams that were once diverse became monocultural—all white, all people of color, all men, or all women.

Without addressing the *isms* that team members had experienced growing up and continued to live by in their segregated communities, the teams reverted to exclusionary behaviors they knew. Although the intent of the organization was to create diverse teams and leverage their talents, they were unable to do so because they had not addressed the oppressive beliefs and behaviors of many of the team members.

THE COST OF DOING BUSINESS
THE OLD WAY

Organization K, a well-respected business services organization, was experiencing high turnover among the young people coming in. The organization hired new MBAs from its list of the best schools, and then expected them to learn the ropes. Before they joined the organization, the new recruits were treated like royalty, literally wined and dined. They met with senior executives and were filled with high expectations.

On arrival, however, they found a very different scenario. Although they had been interviewed at headquarters in a major metropolitan area, many were assigned to offices in small towns. For young people of color, this came as a shock. In their new offices and communities, they found few people who looked like them, and they felt little support from their colleagues, neighbors, supervisors, or headquarters.

Most of these new hires were given positions of little visibility. Although their work often required them to develop presentations for senior officers or other leaders, they were never able to deliver these presentations themselves. Instead, they were instructed to lay low, avoid making waves, and be grateful for the opportunity to gain experience. Needless to say, few of these individuals stayed. They were proud to have the organization listed on their resumes as one of the places they had worked, but they were unwilling to sit in the background and wait their turn. They wanted exciting, meaningful projects now. In exit interviews, many talked about feeling devalued and underutilized.

Even though many of these individuals thrived in high-profile positions in their next organizations, the staid old organization continued to view the high turnover rates among its young recruits, especially people of color, as a necessary weeding-out process. Many of its leaders believed that the conservative, risk-averse, order-followers who remained were "our type of people." Meanwhile, their competitors were thankful for the training and experience that the organization had provided to their new recruits.

When reaching out for new hires or for internal promotions, an organization needs to exercise discipline to identify specifically what needs it hopes to fill and what qualities and competencies will be required for future success. There will always be problems when organizations seek to expand their diversity without seeking to expand their existing skill-sets, or without being able to articulate how the organization's business needs are served by its new candidates.

If current trends continue, many people will be changing jobs and/or organizations every few years. This phenomenon has far-reaching implications for such traditional notions as the career path, the future of the company person and the value of succession planning.

In this kind of high-turnover, serial-employment environment, organizations must not only make recruitment of new talent a mission-critical priority, but also find ways to quickly and productively integrate their new talent into the vital work of the organization. The traditional strategy—"Bring them along slowly. Don't give them anything important to do in the first couple of years."—doesn't work when new people stick around for only a couple of years. This environment also puts a premium on retention strategies. Adding even a single year to a talented person's tenure pays significant dividends. Whether the economic climate is hot or cold, the need to retain talent remains essential.

Organizations must change their cultures if they want to hang on to new talent. The key is to create organizational cultures that welcome, nurture, and develop all their people, whether their differences are visible, cultural or temporal. By contrast, in most organizations, new people are treated as badly as other "outsiders"— women of color, white women, men of color, people with an accent, people with disabilities, and other social identity groups. They are treated with suspicion, mistrust, and fear, alternately hazed and ignored. Before they are accepted into the life and culture of the organization, they are made to prove again and again not only that they can do their jobs, but also that they can fit in.

People create value, therefore they have value. A corollary of this premise is that as people develop, gain experience, and learn new skills, they can create even greater value and become even more valuable. The magazine *Fast Company* often addresses the need for organizations to view people as the creators of value. In its August 2001 issue, an editorial stated, "There is a noble promise at the heart of the new world of business: Everyone has the right to meaningful work, and people who do meaningful work create the most value in the marketplace. . . . Stop trying to change people. Start trying to help them become more of who they already are."

Today's generation sees itself as ready to contribute and grab the baton now. For them, the concept of wait your turn simply does not compute. They consider themselves to be free agents. If one organization won't give them the challenges, responsibilities, and salary they want right now, others surely will. When they leave an organization after a year or two, they take their talent and training out the door, often to the organization's competition.

Organizations need to attract new talent now and for the future. With the global shortage of knowledge workers projected to continue for decades, organizations must position themselves to compete not just for customers and market share, but also for a more talented workforce.

To attract new talent, organizations must create an environment that welcomes new people and enables them to thrive. Companies must prove that theirs is an environment in which new people can develop and succeed by maintaining a population of new people who are developing and succeeding.

Even in organizations that have made large investments in diversity training, the lack of inclusion of new people is startling. It is reflected in the nationwide statistics on employee turnover shown in Table 3.

Table 3: Employee turnover by length of employment

Tenure	0–2 years	3–5 years	10 years	10+ years	Not known
Percent of turnover	72	10	3	4	11

Source: 1999 Thomas Staffing Employee Retention Survey, based on a sample of 953 businesses.

As more and more organizations recognize the value of a diverse workforce, even if only for public relations value, talented people who don't fit the traditional mold—men of color, women of color, white women, lesbians and gays, people with disabilities, and people from other social identity groups—often find themselves the focus of bidding wars. Yet when they accept the winning bid, they may find that their new organization doesn't quite know what to do with them. They may have been recruited to fit into a job or help the organization's image, not to help the organization redefine its way of doing business. After a few months, many of them are ready to move on again, looking for an organization that may actually want them to bring their difference to make a difference.

Turning the tables on such thinking can energize an organization at all levels. Seeking out an individual's differences can create dynamic thinking in the workplace and the marketplace, especially when it is made clear that those differences benefit, and are embraced by, the organization.

Organization L, a rapidly growing technology organization, was struggling to attract a new group of talented people to help sustain its growth. In the organization, managers were competing with each other for the available talent that had already been hired. To encourage people to transfer into their departments, some managers offered extra perks, such as access to flextime and favorable shifts. Some offered promotions and bonuses. One manager focused on making his workgroup more diverse and inclusive. He offered equal access to flextime for all and bonuses based on the entire workgroup's achievements. Instead of bringing in new people as isolated individuals, he brought in cohorts of new people from several social identity groups so they could support each other as new people. He made it everyone's business that all people feel included, and made it clear that they would share individual failures as well as group successes. If one failed, they all failed.

Soon, word circulated throughout the organization that this manager's group was an exciting place to be. While other managers went begging for talent to fill their openings, this manager had a waiting list of many of the highest potential people in the organization. In fact, many were willing to make lateral moves to join this group.

Over a period of time, this workgroup became not only one of the most diverse groups in the organization, but also one of the highest performing groups in the industry. People who had been there a while felt wanted and needed; new people felt valued and included.

Together, they accomplished more than any of them had ever accomplished individually. They were able to build upon what they had in common—a commitment to higher performance and clarity of their mission—and to succeed because of, not in spite of, the differences they brought.

A Two-Way Agreement

If an organization wants people to invest their time, energy and talents in the achievement of its mission, the organization must invest in those people. It is the essence of the new work contract. It is a two-way agreement between employer and employee—or better stated, between team leader and partners.

Organizations must see their people as organizational assets and invest in nurturing those assets by building each person's knowledge, skills, and behavioral effectiveness, while realizing that a talented person may walk out the door on any given day. In this era of free agency, an organization must hope that by supporting people's acquisition of knowledge and skills without many strings attached, treating them with respect, enabling them to do their best work, acknowledging them as whole people with important work, family and personal lives—in other words, by practicing inclusion—it will become the Employer of Choice for its people.

Consider this scenario: A woman who is energized and enthusiastic about joining Company A is told from day one that this is a sink-or-swim organization. At the first staff meeting, she recognizes that she must tone down her excitement as she listens to people discuss, without passion, plans for a new project. Although she has many ideas to contribute, she gets the message that she is too new to contribute; her job is to listen and learn the ropes, to learn to do it the company way. By the end of her first year, she is identified as a good performer who knows how to fit in. She, however, feels as though the very air is being sucked out of her. The organization is still cautious about discussing her career possibilities—they feel it is too soon to commit.

Now imagine this same woman in Company B. From day one she is told by her peers and manager how pleased the company is that she agreed to join them. After having been thoroughly briefed by a diverse cohort of buddies, she is frequently asked by her manager and team members to share her perspectives and ideas. Because she brings fresh eyes to the organization, they say, she can contribute much to improving their functioning and to the development of new ideas and processes. By the end of the first year, her manager tells her that she is a star based on her many contributions and her way of including and working with others. She is told about the high expectations for her career growth and development.

BEING A MAGNET FOR TALENT

Perhaps the truest test of any organization's strategies for leveraging diversity and inclusion is the answer to the question "Given complete freedom to work for any number of organizations, why would the most talented people work for yours?"

To remain competitive, both in the market for customers and the market for people, an organization must become a magnet for talent. Today, the key question many individuals are asking of their organizations is "Are you worthy of my ideas, energy, and commitment?"

High-potential people from diverse backgrounds consider nine key characteristics to be significant in selecting a worthy organization to join (Gans, Katz & Miller, 1998).

The Leaders are worthy of respect and followership

Most talented people join an organization because of its reputation and its leaders. Individuals want to work with leaders who have the knowledge and skills to lead the organization and inspire its people. Leaders need to communicate their ideas, vision, strategies and directions effectively, listen to all people at all levels, and model the values of the organization. People's immediate managers must demonstrate these qualities and competencies as well.

The organization is growing

To grow and develop in today's economy, the organization must be seen as having upside potential. Few people are eager to join a failing or downsizing business. The organization must be positioned for growth in its markets, services, and product development to evoke optimism for a bright future for the organization and its people.

Support is available for work, life, and family integration

The organization's work, life, and family policies must enable its members to fulfill outside responsibilities—such as caring for young children, sick partners or elderly parents, dealing with health-care issues, and pursuing their education—without undo hardship or without jeopardizing their careers. People should not be required to sacrifice their families, their personal lives, or their health for the sake of the organization. The organization must recognize that a person's quality of life is a key factor in her or his ability to contribute. More and more individuals recognize the precarious nature of their careers and will not sacrifice their lives for an organization if there seems to be little offered in return.

People enjoy ample opportunities for continuous growth and development

The organization must give people opportunities, encouragement and support to improve their skills and grow beyond their organizational boxes. The organization needs to work actively to provide internal and external educational, career, and skills enhancement opportunities. It is key that managers be held accountable for enhancing people's growth and development.

The organization fosters a sense of community

A vital element in achieving an inclusion breakthrough is creating a feeling of belonging in the organization. People should experience a broad range of acceptable behaviors in the organization and feel free to operate within and test that range. They should feel special for being members of the organization, acknowledge one another as members, and genuinely like, admire, and respect many of their colleagues, citing their team members as one of the best things about their jobs.

Research indicates that a primary reason for staying in an organization is people's commitment to and investment in their colleagues. A culture committed to an inclusion breakthrough strives to create and leverage a sense of community among all its members.

The environment promotes physical and emotional safety

The organization must provide a safe environment in which to work. People must not be in danger of physical harm from the processes or other people in the workplace. There must also be a clear commitment to emotional safety in the workplace—no harassment, no initiation by hazing, no zings or nibbles (Jamison, 1989). Rather, the culture should support and encourage all people to do their best.

People are treated as business partners

In the truest sense of bring your brains to work, people need to be recognized and treated as partners. Instead of merely being expected to blindly follow orders, people should be afforded respect and trust, based on a tacit assumption that they are working on behalf of the organization's mission and goals, even when they are challenging what has been or what is being proposed. People should be given credit for their unique expertise and supported to bring their knowledge and ideas to the enterprise. They need to be given the opportunity to have their rewards tied to the overall performance of the organization, as well as to team and individual accomplishments through profit-sharing, stock options, bonuses, incentives, and the like.

Communication flows clearly and freely

Information should flow effectively up, down, and across the organization. People feel that they have access to all job-relevant information through an open communications platform that they can access based on their needs and desires. They should be encouraged to use clear, direct and honest communication in all workplace interactions.

Roles and expectations are clearly stated

The organization's expectations of people regarding roles, responsibilities, performance, commitments and rewards need to be clear—what you give, what you get and for how long. To leverage talent, all people who are told that they are competent must be treated as competent and as the right person for their position. People who are not performing up to expectations must be given clear feedback and direction regarding what those expectations are. Then they must be offered the opportunity and support to develop so that they can succeed. If the expectations are not met over time, those people should be asked to leave.

Few organizations have devoted themselves to encouraging or supporting their members' involvement with their families or communities. Few have evolved beyond the view that people are a necessary expense of doing business. Fewer still have made the conceptual leap to see their people as partners and their work culture as needing to be people-centric.

If the rates of pay are reasonably close, a person's attention will fall to job elements that affect her or his potential market value. Further, the affiliations chosen by individuals today will be those most consistent with the values they hold.

A critical part of leveraging a diverse workforce is ensuring that the organization is seen as a worthy organization. By becoming a worthy organization for all people, organizations give people a reason to stay and contribute. When everyone experiences support at all levels, they return that support with productivity and energy many times over. The organization can also gain access to unprecedented synergies derived from previously suppressed interactions between differing sets of perspectives, talents, problem-solving styles, and experience.

By undertaking an inclusion breakthrough and creating an environment in which all people are encouraged and supported to do their best work, individually and collectively, an organization sets itself up to become the magnet for talent upon which its future depends.

Utilizing both new talent and traditional talent leads to greater innovation in an organization's products and services. By having and leveraging diversity, an organization has more resources and options and becomes less vulnerable to outside threat. It also enhances the interactions with stakeholders in the community. When focused on diversity in the box—expecting everyone to fit inside limits—the capability to create new products and services and to innovate is stilted.

Community and Social Responsibility

In the past few years, many organizations have come to recognize the strategic advantage of being socially responsible and investing in their local communities. Just as the new implied workforce contract calls for a two-way investment, an organization's relationship with the community must also be reciprocal.

An effective inclusion breakthrough strategy cannot focus solely within the walls of the organization. To thrive, companies must develop beneficial partnerships with the people, organizations, and communities that provide them with their workforce, customers, suppliers, and distributors. They need healthy communities in which talented people will choose to live—communities with effective schools, breathable air, safe drinking water, and uncontaminated food. They need a healthy overall economy in which their products and services can find thriving markets. They need a social and a physical environment that will sustain them over the long haul, not just until the day after the next quarter's financial reports are posted.

There are almost as many meanings to being a socially responsible enterprise as there are organizations. For some, it might mean raising the pay scale from minimum wage to a livable wage. It might mean investing in the community for sound schools or working

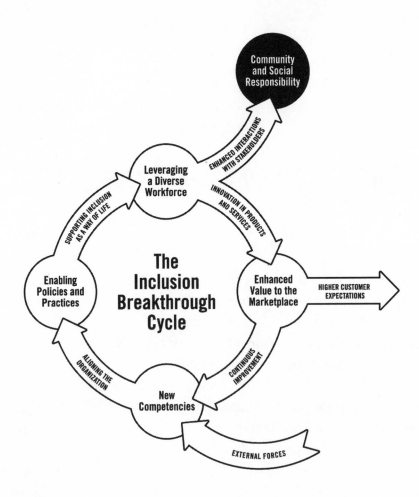

with police and government officials for a safe community. For others, it might mean improving environmental practices.

A growing, worldwide movement holds organizations, especially large corporations, accountable for the effect they have on the world around them. In response, many companies are addressing their environmental and social policies and practices, including the effect they have on various social identity groups in the communities they serve.

In addressing a worldwide Mobil diversity forum in 1999, Lou Noto, former CEO of Mobil, said, "Successful organizations need successful communities. You cannot have a viable organization if you do not have a viable community." Accordingly, many organizations have taken the notion of investing in the local community to heart.

Some organizations demand a one-way investment *from* the community, seeking tax breaks and government-backed financial incentives for remaining or relocating in a specific region. In offering their loyalty to the highest bidder, but only for as long as the incentives last, they often receive the same kind of loyalty in return. Other organizations derive greater long-term benefits by making extended investments in the infrastructure of the community, helping improve its recreational, educational, and healthcare facilities. In doing so, they help make the community a more attractive place for people to live and work. And, in addition to improving the community's standard of living, they improve the quality of life of their workforce, customers, and business partners.

Progressive and forward-thinking business leaders are looking at all the communities where their organizations' facilities are located, not just affluent communities but also those struggling to survive. They are seeing investment in these communities not as a handout or public relations ploy but as a hard-edged necessity. As Whirlpool CEO David Whitwam said at a meeting of Michigan's Council for World Class Communities, "Unless our communities can attract the kind of people we want working in our company, our company cannot survive."

How Much Will it Cost?

Many organizations are finding that socially responsible policies and actions do not necessarily cost more than pursuing a profit-only strategy. In fact, the return often grows when an organization becomes more responsive to the needs of its community. By reducing waste, some organizations have reduced the cost of both their raw materials and their waste disposal. By making investments in improved physical working conditions, some organizations have been rewarded with major reductions in absenteeism and increases in productivity.

In the following speech excerpt, an oil company executive describes the results of his company's commitment to reducing greenhouse gases (Browne, 2001):

> "In the United States, venting accounts for almost 60 percent of all the methane which is emitted by our gas business in the Western states. To reduce that, we have a project underway to control emissions from all wells in the areas of the Greater Green River and the San Juan basin.
>
> "This is not an easy project, but we've now found that with an investment of $1.4 million we can save more than 20,000 tons of methane a year, which has the greenhouse effect of nearly half a million tons of carbon dioxide.
>
> "And of course the methane can now be sold—turning what began as an environmental project into something that is also good profitable business.
>
> "Reducing emissions was the first goal. The second was to demonstrate that we could create an internal trading system which would allow us to meet our target at the lowest possible cost by allocating the resources to the places where they would have most effect . . . meeting the target not by requiring everyone to cut emissions by 10 percent, but by putting a monetary value on each unit and encouraging the whole internal team to cooperate in delivering the target at the lowest cost."

Not only can socially responsible business strategies help profitability, they can also attract investment. A number of high-performing, green mutual funds select stocks based on companies' environmental policies and performance. In some market sectors, in fact, green companies outperform their competitors.

The March 2001 issue of *Tomorrow Essentials* quotes an Innovest Strategic Value Advisors report: "Water companies with the best environmental ratings also offer the soundest financial prospects." The report cites companies, such as Anglia Water and Severn Trent of the United Kingdom and France's Vivendi Universal, that out-performed other industry companies by an average of 4.5 percent over the past three years. The report notes that these types of companies excel at developing cost-effective technologies in response to environmentally driven regulations.

The key is tying socially responsible investing to corporate social responsibility. Amy Domini, founder of Domini Social Equity Fund, put it this way (Domini, 2001):

> "The purpose of Socially Responsible Investing is to harness our investments toward creating a more just and sustainable economic system.
>
> "Domini seeks to invest in companies with positive records in community involvement, the environment, employee relations and diversity.
>
> "Social investors do not support detrimental social and environmental practices. We believe the potential liabilities associated with such practices will likely have adverse impact on stock performance over the long term; companies with strong employee relations generally enjoy higher morale and productivity, reduced absenteeism, and lower hiring, training, and turnover costs. . . . Corporate social responsibility is a superior business strategy; companies with strong environmental profiles enjoy lower energy costs, reduced risk, lower costs of capital, and enhanced reputations in the marketplace.
>
> "Over the past decade the notions of socially responsible investing and corporate social responsibility have taken hold. The next decade must be about transforming the system itself—ushering in a new, more sustainable and humane form of capitalism."

Socially responsible investment funds are raising the bar on organizations. The issue of social responsibility is being extended beyond environmental concerns to issues of diversity and inclusion. That higher bar is another reason why organizations are pursuing inclusion breakthrough strategies. Investors and funds are examining organizations based not only on their environmental records, but also on their policies and practices with respect to leveraging diversity and their treatment of all people.

Business leaders are also beginning to recognize that all people deserve a livable wage: salaries that allow them to own houses and raise families in the communities where they work. Some cite a moral imperative; others are taking up the cause in the name of sustainability. They believe that for businesses to survive and thrive, they must support their communities by ensuring that the people in them can support themselves and their families. Businesses looking to make an inclusion breakthrough, seeing their people as their greatest assets, are beginning to shift the equation to make sure that they retain and support those assets.

BEYOND PHILANTHROPY: VOLUNTEERISM AND PARTNERSHIPS

Organizations that hold a diversity in a box perspective often position their external diversity-related efforts as philanthropy. This frames the issues and opportunities as handouts to specific social identity groups, thereby diminishing both the people and the effort and subverting the potential advantages of an inclusion breakthrough. It also renders the commitment to diversity as a good-times-only, optional program. Charity, after all, is given only when one can afford it. It is a gift from the more fortunate to the less fortunate, a subtraction from a surplus—not an essential investment of working capital.

All organizations claim to make efforts to give back to the community, but few go beyond token attempts. The key is to establish the organization as part of the community in which it operates. Investing in and financially partnering with the community directly affect the lives of the people in the community and do more than help public relations; they establish the organization as one committed to its surroundings. In turn, the benefits of those efforts will bounce back to the organization, providing an improved living and working environment for all.

Individuals can do this as well. Baby boomers and Generation Xers want more out of life than what exists within the walls of their workplace. Many boomers want to rekindle the values of the 1960s to help make the world a better place. Many Gen Xers feel that their parents' materialism has led to empty lives. A vital element of an inclusion breakthrough strategy is seizing the opportunity to give talented people reasons to stay, including meeting their need to give something back.

Organizations are also extending their inclusion breakthrough to volunteerism, and establishing real and meaningful partnerships with various ethnic and diverse sectors of their communities and local businesses.

Organization M, a customer-service-oriented company in a predominantly Latino community, was committed to increasing its population of Latinos and Latinas as part of its inclusion breakthrough strategy. The senior executives and its Diversity and Inclusion Task Force decided that the best approach for achieving this goal was to become better known as a good place for Latinos and Latinas to work. Toward that end, they created a strategic volunteerism program that sent people from the organization out to tutor in the community's schools, which helped parents and students get to know the organization. Some of this time was during working hours, and people were reimbursed as part of the organization's contribution to the efforts. To directly support the community-volunteerism effort, the organization developed a training program for people who were interested in sitting on local nonprofit boards, and supported them with time and donations when they were elected. The organization also worked with the region's Chamber of Commerce, made a point of selecting local suppliers from a diverse pool, and provided support advertising to local small businesses owned by people of color.

Extending the reach of the program to its business partners, the organization instructed the local temporary employment agency—the entry point to the organization for many people—that it wanted individuals selected from a diverse talent pool. In this way, it tied its external outreach activities to its internal inclusion breakthrough strategy. The outcome was that over an 18-month period, not only did the organization receive an award from the Hispanic Chamber of Commerce, but it also began to be known as an employer of choice, as more Latinos and Latinas joined the organization at all levels.

Volunteerism and activities such as Make a Difference Days allow people to do community-focused activities that reconnect them to their values, their communities, and their full selves. By supporting these kinds of activities, organizations support their people and their communities in ways that enrich everyone involved.

People whose employers support their community-focused activities feel good about themselves, good about their jobs, and proud to be part of a community-minded enterprise. The community benefits from these added energies and resources, and the people in the community develop a higher regard for the sponsoring organization. All this can help influence customer decisions, supplier contracts, civil regulations and career seekers.

LONG-TERM BENEFITS

According to an editorial in the March 2001 *Harvard Management Update*, community involvement has become a strategic imperative for many organizations. United States corporations spend a total of $3 billion annually on community involvement programs, and they are continually seeking ways to make that investment more effective with respect to business goals. For instance, online volunteer matching and placement services such as VolunteerMatch Corporate have attracted major corporate clients, including Bank of America, Coca-Cola, Dell Computer, Levi Strauss, and Nike.

However, these are not just one-way investments. To thrive, organizations need their surrounding communities to thrive as well. The communities, after all, are the organizations' primary source of people, customers, suppliers, distributors, partners, and investors. The organization and the community must feed one another if they both are to profit from geographic codependence.

Another element of social responsibility is ensuring that local businesses are successful—making a commitment to develop partnerships with local entrepreneurs to strengthen the community, directing money back into the community, building partnerships with businesses that are socially responsible, and insuring that there is collective action to affect the environment beyond the reach of the organization for the betterment of all.

Enhanced Value to the Marketplace

As organizations start to reach out to a wider spectrum of customers, many continue to do so from a perspective that makes representation the goal and diversity something to be managed, tolerated, or used as a tool to highlight certain opportunities. Some organizations may consider the diverse segments of the marketplace as niches rather than as core to business success, and see diversity through the lens of the box, as ancillary and not central to the organizations' definition of the marketplace.

One common misconception of the expanding opportunities offered by a diverse marketplace is that these opportunities exist primarily in other countries. Too often, a focus on global diversity overlooks the chance to capitalize on the diversity that exists in the organization's home country.

There is an enormous, untapped opportunity to serve African American markets, the Latino and Asian American markets—the two fastest-growing demographic market segments in the United States—the lesbian and gay markets, the deaf culture market, the women's market, and other social-identity-group markets. Just as organizations have segmented their traditional market—white men based on age, education, and income—there is an enormous benefit

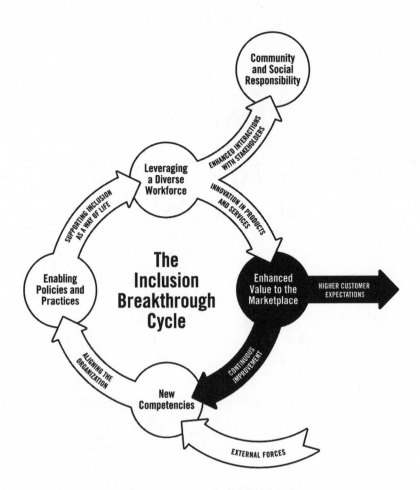

to delve deeper into the differentiation of populations and to see the market opportunities waiting to be explored.

After deciding that Canada was its best growth market, Organization N, a large US-based packaged-goods organization, began planning a major effort to develop business there. Organization N's leaders knew this would be an expensive effort that would require large capital expenditures to establish new distribution networks, but Canada was closer than many other countries they considered.

Then the vice president who was driving this northward push left Organization N. His replacement from outside the company had a different perspective on the situation. He suggested that the familiar color (mostly white) and ethnicity (mostly European) of Canada's population had unduly influenced his predecessor's decision to expand into Canada. In his first week on the job, he said again and again, "There are more Hispanics in the United States than there are Canadians in Canada." Organization N almost overlooked an opportunity to address an even larger potential market in its current distribution network, without incurring the expenses of setting up new distribution systems and developing new partnerships with retail businesses and suppliers in a new country.

Based on his previous experience, the new vice president believed that Organization N could take advantage of a significant opportunity in this so-called new marketplace. The Canadian strategy was tabled and the Hispanic marketing effort was launched. As a result, Organization N increased sales more than 20 percent in the first year of this stay-at-home market-expansion strategy.

Untapped identity group markets offer terrific opportunities for any organization seeking to expand its customer base and talent pool. But recognizing that none of these seemingly narrow markets is monolithic can reap even greater opportunities. Each embodies a range of individual tastes, desires and needs. No one is a member of a single identity group. Categorizing people as such is a certain prescription for business failure.

Organizations that are good at interacting and partnering with people of different social identity groups and the diverse elements in each identity group are in the best position to connect with these market segments. But to make the most of this advantage, people with those competencies must be in positions of authority and influence, included in the core processes of the organization, and able to provide input into organizational policies and practices.

This does not mean that a business that primarily sells to Latino and Latina Americans must be run solely by Latino and Latina Americans or that all decision-makers in a baby-food company must be mothers or fathers. It does mean that organizations with the competencies to understand, think and live in an identity group's experience will have a significant advantage over traditional monocultural organizations when it comes to capturing a share of that identity group's business.

Organizations and people who are able to translate those competencies into the design, delivery, and marketing of their products and services will be the big winners in the marketplace of today and tomorrow. They will lead their industries in the inclusion breakthrough that is required for success.

Those who continue to believe that they can gain the benefits of diversity only by being sensitive to diversity issues, contributing to charities, and hiring from a particular social identity group for public relations purposes will lose the competition for the increasingly diverse national and global marketplace.

INCREASING CUSTOMER EXPECTATIONS RAISES THE BAR FOR EVERYONE

In a global economy that increasingly has become a buyers' market, the buyers have become increasingly more sophisticated and demanding. Each organization that incorporates elements of an inclusion breakthrough into its marketing and customer-service practices gains a competitive edge over organizations that haven't embraced those elements. Social identity groups develop preferences and loyalties for organizations that best serve their interests and turn away from organizations that don't.

Continuing to operate in the same old ways guarantees the loss of entire groups of customers. The bar is being raised continuously. The customer-focus movement has been a response to the buyers' market economy. The extension of this to understanding and supporting diversity is critical for organizational success—customers count, and they demand to be counted. Organizations such Rainbow/PUSH and many others have led boycotts of businesses whose policies and practices seem to discriminate against African Americans and other social identity groups.

Customers of all identity groups are realizing the power of their money. They are making choices about what products and services to purchase based not only on quality and price but also on organizational practices. Given a choice between otherwise equal products, many people choose the ones made by organizations they perceive to be more aligned with their values, more responsive to their needs as customers, and more willing to treat them with respect as individuals and identity-group members.

It takes more than simply not discriminating in today's marketplace to win over loyal customers. Capitalizing on an inclusion breakthrough strategy requires actively engaging with the diversity of the community, workforce and marketplace to create and deliver value.

SCRATCH THAT NICHE

As recently as the 1970s, most baby-food companies still had men making all the key product-development and marketing decisions. They were missing the capability to reach out compellingly to the mothers who actually shopped for their products. As long as all baby-food companies remained equally insensitive to the range of needs and desires of their niche, this was not a survival issue.

When Organization O started conducting focus groups with mothers to learn about product preferences, their success in the marketplace began to shift. The organization that conducted the research started producing baby food that was more highly valued by their consumers. And when they hired women who were mothers to help them interpret the focus group data and develop new product and packaging options, they started a breakthrough strategy for the rest of the industry to follow.

The expanding market power of individual identity groups has led to a proliferation of niche businesses. In fact, during the 1990s, an organization's capability to customize products and services to fit a narrow segment of the market seemed to be the textbook key to success.

In fact, the best way to pursue a niche market is to understand its unique qualities. Many of the failed dot-coms were niche businesses that identified an unfilled need and sought to exploit it through narrow-focus customization. Many ultimately found that their focus was too narrow.

Knowing the niche is more than identifying the niche. Some members of the organization must have the competencies to understand the niche as if they were members. Those competencies need to be available to a critical mass of the people in the organization.

Before car manufacturers began hiring women as automotive engineers and designers, making a car woman friendly meant putting a lighted vanity mirror in the passenger-seat visor and offering pink as one of the color options. Today, women are beginning to achieve a degree of acceptance in automotive-design circles, and their influence is beginning to have an effect. In most new cars, the handle for adjusting the driver's seat has been moved from between the legs to the side of the seat, where it's more convenient for a driver who is wearing a skirt. Minivans are being restructured to be more family-friendly, with VCRs and headphones for children. Even the running boards on trucks are being adjusted so that shorter people, and skirt-wearing people can more easily get into them.

For decades, Organization P, a major canned-food company, had developed and marketed its products for the average consumer. In the post-baby-boom era, when the United States population started to level out, the organization's sales also flattened. Then an African American woman took over product development. Her background and experience resulted in the emergence of new products and new customers. Cornbread, vegetables with spices, and commercials in different languages breathed new life into the organization and

opened up new markets, new products and—most important—
steadily increasing sales.

However, if an organization decides it wants to target Asians, for
example, in its marketing effort, it cannot simply hire some Asian
people to create an ad campaign. Just because a person is Asian or
Asian American doesn't mean that person can represent all Asians or
Asian Americans. An organization needs varied perspectives and
voices at the table, particularly at the decision-making table. Ideally,
all of them will be sensitive to and knowledgeable about the market
segment being addressed, with the competencies needed to distin-
guish between activities that are merely attention-getting or offensive and what is respectful and will be experienced as inclusive by
the group.

Hiring, including and empowering members of a particular social
identity group are not enough to make an inclusion breakthrough.
Just hiring lesbians and gays will not enable an organization to
market successfully to lesbians and gays. The organization will also
need its heterosexual people to be able to connect with and understand its lesbian and gay customers. One of the causes of many lawsuits against companies accused of producing offensive ads is that
their advertising staff doesn't have expertise to address today's
diverse marketplace.

Some organizations limit their growth by not including the total
available marketplace. For example, based on the common assumption that African Americans are poor and therefore don't make viable
customers, a major computer manufacturer mistakenly assumed that
its primary market was 40-year-old white men. Many people inside
United States-based organizations make similar errors because they
don't know anything about the lifestyles, services, or product needs
of other cultures, even in the United States. These issues plague
organizations that are trying to do business globally as well.

PARTNERING FOR SUCCESS

For many organizations, creating international, regional, and local partnerships is a key to success. An organization will find it much easier and more economical to gain the necessary understanding of local customs and culture in new markets by engaging the assistance of people with intimate knowledge of those markets. That requires *partnership* based on mutual respect and appreciation, in which people and organizations work together productively and cooperatively to establish and pursue common interests and create mutual value. For a global organization, it is a prerequisite of doing business to establish a local presence, to put into place leaders from the particular locations, and to be seen as a part of the host countries' cultures and traditions.

No organization will succeed in the inner city or with racial, ethnic, or other identity groups without forming local partnerships with those groups.

Capitalizing on diverse partnerships with people different than the dominant group will be the challenge for organizations looking to compete on a global scale in the twenty-first century and beyond. This requires a new set of skills, interactions and competencies:

- Recognizing the value of a partnership by understanding that each partner brings value to the table and is a valuable source of intelligence and judgment.

- Ensuring that each partner has some stake and some gain to be made from the collaboration.

- Listening with an open mind to the partners' point of view, learning about their context and what potential customers need, and not assuming the organization's opinions must take precedence but rather that local people know best what is needed.

- Thinking outside the box. The question is not, "How do we apply what we already have to this setting?" Rather, it is, "How do we pursue new opportunities in the cultural context that is right for us, our local partners and the customers we want to serve?"

- Developing talent globally and locally.

AN EXPANDED VIEW OF CUSTOMERS

To create an inclusion breakthrough, organizations must develop a whole new view of who their customers are, what services and products to develop for them, and how to reach those markets through marketing and advertising. This requires nothing short of transforming their businesses and their way of doing things. It means being able to think about differentiation of customer needs as part of the whole and not only as ancillary segments. It means customization of marketing as standard operating procedure and redefining who is incorporated in the mass market.

Organizations are just beginning to realize the potential gains that will result from making an inclusion breakthrough in the marketplace. The organizations that cannot make this leap will not succeed. They will find their markets flat with few growth opportunities.

Making a breakthrough also means adopting a different approach to being a global organization, rethinking who and what the marketplace is, and realizing that it does not mean simply exporting products to another country or changing a few words in an ad. It means understanding the local context, developing partnerships for success and accepting the shifts of power and control that ensue.

A United States-based diaper manufacturer tried to expand its marketing reach into the Middle East with an advertising campaign featuring a standard "Before and After" example of its product's benefits. The ads and product packaging showed side-by-side pictures of a crying baby on the left, a smiling, happy baby on the right, and a close-up of the manufacturer's diaper in the middle. Unfortunately, the manufacturer's marketing people did not consider that the people in the targeted countries read right-to-left rather than left-to-right, which gave the exact opposite message they intended. Lack of understanding of local context led to lack of sales.

Creating an inclusion breakthrough means redefining who is included and leveraging the thinking of all members of the organization to more powerfully affect the delivery of services and products to an ever-changing marketplace.

Getting to a breakthrough means a whole new way of thinking about business—new ways of engaging customers, new ways of creating products and delivering value to customers. The breakthrough requires a new dynamic engagement of a diverse group of people thinking about a dynamic marketplace.

Unleashing the real power of diversity is not about just adding on to business as usual—there is no such thing as steady state. The inclusion breakthrough is about continuous improvement and continuous change, the capability to respond to an ever-shifting and continually changing environment, and having a wealth of resources capable of responding to that environment. And it continually raises the bar—as customers receive more, they expect more from both the organization and others they come in contact with, demanding that organizations meet and exceed their expectations. Thus, *the new bar becomes the new status quo*. These new demands become the impetus for change—driving the organization toward a new set of demands and opportunities.

PART THREE

Creating an Inclusion Breakthrough

Every organization is different. A rigid formula for change cannot be applied successfully. The methodology for an inclusion breakthrough is designed to be not a road map, but a series of signposts. The route each organization takes depends on its size, hierarchy, infrastructure, people, leadership, and history. It provides tools for identifying themes and issues that prevent the people of an organization from doing their best work. And it offers guidelines for addressing those issues in ways that will lead to sustainable success. Ultimately, it is designed to create an inclusion breakthrough—an environment in which every member of the organization can add value and enhance the organization's performance and competitive advantage for today and tomorrow.

The methodology is composed of four phases, as shown in Table 4: building a platform for change; creating momentum; making diversity and inclusion a way of life; and leveraging learning and challenging the new status quo.

Table 4: The KJCG methodology for an inclusion breakthrough

INTEGRATION INTO ORGANIZATIONAL CORE WORK PROCESSES				MANAGEMENT PLANS, POLICIES AND PRACTICES ALIGNMENT
PHASE I: BUILDING THE PLATFORM FOR CHANGE				
• Position effort to be a Way of Life • Establish the Organizational Imperative for the culture change	• Undertake organizational assessment, i.e., "Giving Voice" sessions • Begin Education and alignment of senior leaders	• Feedback session with learning partners • Identify internal leadership for the change effort	• Take immediate actions in areas that need attention and/or "make a statement" about the commitment to the Inclusion Breakthrough	
PHASE II: CREATING MOMENTUM				
• Develop initial 12- to 18-month plan	• Implement aggressive efforts to engage, inform and enroll the people of the organization • Develop a critical mass of Agents of Change	• Begin education to create new competencies for senior leaders, managers, individual contributors • Create processes to address blatant or subtle discrimination/ barriers	• Support networks, mentoring, coaching and buddy systems • Identify and begin work in "Pockets of Readiness"	
PHASE III: MAKING DIVERSITY AND INCLUSION A WAY OF LIFE				
• Expand the initial plan to a long-term strategic plan that integrates and partners with all change initiatives	• Formalize accountability for living the competencies in the new culture (scorecards & other tools) • Baseline diversity and inclusion into all education, training and programs	• Implement incentives and rewards to support the Inclusion Breakthrough and to create organizational pull • Enhance performance feedback systems to support the new culture	• Involve stakeholders (e.g., suppliers, joint ventures, acquisitions, community, board members)	
PHASE IV: LEVERAGING LEARNING AND CHALLENGING THE NEW STATUS QUO				
• Reassess organization to identify progress and gaps • Reassess how the work of the organization is done	• Communicate accomplishments and success practices internally and externally	• Identify and address areas that will support higher and higher performance	• Continuously improve the change process	

Although we present the phases sequentially, the components need not be implemented in this manner. Whereas some actions and strategies may be implemented only after certain resources and competencies have been developed, others may be carried out simultaneously. The methodology is flexible and adaptable to the needs of each organization. In different organizations, different interventions may be required at different stages, and some parts of some organizations will move at different paces. Therefore, those implementing the methodology must be flexible and adaptable as well.

Organizations that have made long-term commitments to implementing these breakthrough strategies have seen substantive, measurable, and positive changes, including reduced employee turnover, improved customer satisfaction, faster and more effective customer service, increased market share, successful penetration into new markets, and increased productivity. From front-line people to CEOs, people have also reported new levels of innovation, enthusiasm, commitment, job satisfaction, belonging, and contribution.

These strategies are predicated on four essential building blocks of effective change:

- **Leverage:** Find and develop the most effective actions and points of opportunity to gain the maximum payoff from each action undertaken. Work to enhance the strengths of the organization rather than spending time on points of resistance.

- **Linkage:** Coordinate and connect all organizational initiatives and activities so that they work together to create a total that is greater than the sum of its parts.

- **Leadership:** Equip both formal and informal leaders of the organization with the education and skills training needed to live and model an organizational culture that leverages diversity and builds inclusion. Hold each person accountable for her or his actions–making inclusion a way of life.

- **Learning:** Recognize the process of change as an act of continuous discovery. Understand that making mistakes is part of the learning process.

Building the Platform
for Change

Phase I of the technology for creating an inclusion breakthrough focuses on identifying, developing, and aligning resources and positioning the effort for implementation. It is the time for finding allies and partners and for laying the groundwork for change. In many ways, the most difficult part of the effort occurs before ever moving to the Phase I action items (see Table 5). Whether as an individual or as a group, taking the career-threatening risk of standing up and advocating for change requires a great deal of courage. That is what is required before real change can begin.

POSITION THE EFFORT TO BE A WAY OF LIFE

Change can start anywhere in an organization: in middle management, among line workers or in the Human Resources department. But for any change effort to be effective, have a lasting effect on an organization and be truly transforming—in other words, to be an inclusion breakthrough—it must be led and modeled from the top. Only the organization's senior executives can provide the commitment, resources, and credibility required to convince people in the organization to stop behaving in the ways they have always behaved and to start adopting new, unfamiliar ways that may initially feel awkward, embarrassing, and risky. Unless senior executives live the

139

Table 5: Phase I of the KJCG methodology for an inclusion breakthrough

PHASE I: BUILDING THE PLATFORM FOR CHANGE			
• Position effort to be a Way of Life • Establish the Organizational Imperative for the culture change	• Undertake organizational assessment, i.e., "Giving Voice" sessions • Begin Education and alignment of senior leaders	• Feedback session with learning partners • Identify internal leadership for the change effort	• Take immediate actions in areas that need attention and/or "make a statement" about the commitment to the Inclusion Breakthrough

behaviors, values and attitudes of the inclusion breakthrough as the organization's new way of life, the rest of the organization will continue to follow the old ways.

The source of a culture change effort varies greatly from organization to organization. Regardless of where it comes from, for the change to take hold, it must proceed as a process of enrollment. Until senior executives are enrolled, the rest of the organization will not feel the safety or urgency to follow. Senior executives and other leaders must understand why the inclusion breakthrough is mission critical and they must begin to develop the understandings and behaviors that engage and enroll others.

When an organization is serious about undertaking an inclusion breakthrough, often the first step is to take stock of how its leaders are positioning the inclusion breakthrough to become a way of life (as illustrated in Figure 3, which appears in Chapter 2). The change cannot be seen as a social program. It must be connected to the organization's business strategy. It must be described and modeled by the organization's senior leadership team as the way it will conduct business from now on.

ESTABLISH AN ORGANIZATIONAL IMPERATIVE

To engage senior executives in the strategic culture change required for an inclusion breakthrough, it is vital to build a framework that everyone can understand.

The *organizational imperative* must state clearly how transforming the old culture and ways of operating and shifting to a new way of business will benefit the organization and each individual. Three critical components of an effective organizational imperative are as follows:

- Tell the story of all the factors that have changed—such as the environment, the marketplace, the needs and expectations of individuals and of the organization—and what is driving the organization to make an inclusion breakthrough process necessary.

- Announce a clear statement of the imperative: what is to be gained and why it is necessary for the organization's survival and success.

- Give examples of costs and missed opportunities incurred by the old ways of operating and old culture, contrasted with examples of expected organizational and personal successes likely to result from living the new culture.

Organization Q was well known for its great people and great products, which for years consisted of name-brand food products that were household staples across the United States. Organization Q was known as one of the top places to work long before those listings were headlined in Fortune, Inc., and other publications. Yet in recent years, Organization Q was struggling. As their competitors grew, Organization Q's growth was flat. Although many people came to work there and ended up staying for many years, it seemed that the brands and the people were stagnating. It was becoming harder and harder to attract new talent—young, diverse, creative and inspired people who brought more diversity to the organization.

The organization invested heavily and tried many new programs to spur product development and create innovative teams, but without much luck. Organization Q even trained people in six sigma to eliminate waste and improve quality performance. But while the organization was focusing on creating greater efficiencies, it was actually moving further away from innovation.

Senior executives began to realize that to jump-start the old corporation toward new growth, it needed a major breakthrough, not incremental change. The environment and the landscape had changed since Organization Q's glory days. In the marketplace, Organization Q faced increased competition. In the community, which once had a fairly balanced diversity, there had emerged two separate communities—one mostly white and affluent and one primarily African American (with an emerging Latino population) and less affluent. This change in the community affected the diversity of talent Organization Q could attract from outside the area. And in a global climate of downsized workforces and reduced profit margins, people still expected the organization to take care of them, and assumed they would retire from the organization after a safe and protected 30-plus-year career.

It was time to reawaken the organization, its products and its people. The organizational imperative for an inclusion breakthrough exposed the need to dramatically change the very rules of the corporation and how it operated. Senior executives, with the assistance of a diverse cross-functional team, formulated the imperative and then embarked on a vigorous campaign to get the word out about the need for change and what people could expect in the days and months ahead.

The imperative focused on three key business areas in which Organization Q was in crisis:

- **Products:** The presence of established brands was diminishing, and it had not had a significant win with a new product in several years. There was a clear need to change its processes and create new winning products. This was a must for Organization Q's survival.

- **People:** Organization Q acknowledged the importance of the loyalty of its people, but now it was calling on them to do more. New people, employee competencies, greater diversity of thought, and more innovation were now critical to the success of the organization. People had to be better educated and develop new skill sets, while utilizing their different backgrounds, perspectives, and talents to spur greater creativity and innovation.

- **Community:** Critical to the organization's success was creating a sustainable, supportive community in which all employees, contractors, and their families could thrive. The organization committed substantial resources to transforming its relationship with the local community and investing in a diverse local supplier base. For the organization to prosper, it needed a sustainable environment for its members and to break down the barriers that existed in the community that made it a less-than-desirable place to live for segments of Organization Q's people.

Through the imperative, Organization Q made it clear that it was in each person's self-interest to support such a transformation, for the very survival of the organization was at stake. If everyone could not succeed, no one would. Organization Q's organizational imperative laid the groundwork for positive change.

To achieve buy-in from the organization's senior leadership, it may be necessary to create a preliminary organizational imperative, based on external trends and a general knowledge of the organization. Later, after a thorough organizational assessment—which examines an organization's policies, practices, aspirations, and interactions—this preliminary document can be revised for presentation to the organization as a whole, using the more specific information derived from the assessment. And as more and more people become involved in the breakthrough process, the imperative gets richer and more defined as individuals begin to see for themselves how their function and operation benefits through their effort.

In one organization, an internal change agent who was attempting to create an inclusion breakthrough drafted a preliminary organizational imperative and presented it to her division head. By increasing the division's competencies for practicing inclusive behaviors, productivity would be improved and employee turnover would be reduced.

The division head supported the initiative, but felt that the organizational imperative needed to address additional issues to gain approval from the management committee. With the division head's input, the document was revised to include anticipated improvements in customer service and synergies with the organization's other divisions. After it was presented to the management committee, the document was again revised for presentation to the CEO, this time with the management committee's input. The committee suggested that it include additional benefits, such as improved relations with suppliers and distributors, and an enhanced reputation as an employer of choice.

In each case, the organizational imperative was modified to achieve buy-in on the need for culture change from the next level of management. Therefore, the imperative was not a static document but a vehicle to start the conversation about why and how an inclusion breakthrough would benefit the organization.

The CEO directed the formation of the Advisory Council for Diversity and Inclusion, which oversaw the further revision of the organizational imperative, including data from a business survey and culture audit of the organization in its organizational assessment. This final document was then presented to the entire membership of the organization through written communications, a series of follow-up forums, and videos. Under the banner of "A New Company—A New Culture," the first collaborative step of the inclusion breakthrough strategy took hold.

UNDERTAKE AN ORGANIZATIONAL ASSESSMENT

The *organizational assessment* is a careful study of the organization— its culture, opportunities, challenges, long-term potential and possibilities for maximizing performance. It must focus on providing a very honest straight talk understanding of the organization. It also identifies what people need from the organization to contribute more effectively to its current and future success, what people need to do their best work and what the organization needs from them. One factor is hearing what the people see as the organizational opportunities and barriers. This process is a critical starting point in the development of a comprehensive, organization-specific strategy. However, because each organization is at a different starting point, an off-the-shelf approach will not do.

The purpose of the organizational assessment is threefold:

- To provide data about the current culture and capabilities of the organization

- To lay the groundwork for creating the comprehensive strategy required for an inclusion breakthrough, including the framing and refining of the organizational imperative

- To establish a baseline for future measurements of the change effort's progress and to provide a benchmark for comparing the organization's practices with others

The organizational assessment is useful as more than just a diagnostic tool. It is also a highly effective tool for initiating change and building momentum. In this sense, the organizational assessment is an intervention. The interviewing and data-gathering process focuses the attention of the organization's people on such issues as organizational performance, inclusion, leveraging diversity, and culture change. It creates a forum in which people can think and talk about their concerns and their hopes. It sends a message that their voices and perspectives are important to the senior leaders of the organization and are a key resource in determining the organization's direction and future success.

People who participate in the assessment focus group sessions, called Giving Voice sessions, often assume active roles in the change process. Many feel a sense of responsibility and ownership for the changes they have helped shape and want to continue to be involved.

In larger organizations, a full and accurate picture can be achieved by surveying 20 to 30 percent of the people, as long as all major demographic and social identity groups and key functions are included. In organizations of fewer than 500 people, everyone should be included in the data-gathering process. The size of the sample and the thoroughness of the organizational assessment are critical for accuracy and establishing the credibility of the assessment's data, key findings, and the path forward.

The focus groups, when conducted with homogenous groupings of people, provide a forum for hearing all the different voices of the organization. Examples of such groupings include hourly workers, Asian managers, Latino technicians, individuals under age 30, and people who have been with the organization for 20 or more years.

A key part of each focus group is a survey questionnaire that provides extensive demographic information to uncover what is true of all groups and where there are differences. The questionnaire focuses on three key areas:

- **High performance:** The extent to which people see the relationship of their work to the achievement of organizational goals, and the degree of alignment in the organization with respect to mission, vision, strategies, values, culture, and policies

- **Leveraging diversity:** The extent to which people's talents, abilities, and skills are utilized in the organization and how different social identity groups' abilities and perspectives are included.

- **Inclusion:** The extent to which individuals feel a sense of belonging and inclusive behaviors are part of the day-to-day life in the organization.

The goal of the written survey is to add to the anecdotal focus group data clear, quantifiable statements about the current state and future needs of the organization. The combination of quantitative and qualitative data allows for a comprehensive understanding of the issues faced by the organization and its people, as well as a solid platform for developing a path forward.

Giving Voice sessions are an important intervention in the organization. Because these sessions are presented to the organization as data gathering that will lead to action, the focus groups help get the people and the leadership of the organization ready for change. If the leaders do not act or do not communicate the outcomes of the feedback, they lose an important opportunity to create a platform for change and run the risk of setting their effort back. An assessment should not be conducted unless senior leaders are positioned and willing to act on the data.

Organization R was conducting Giving Voice focus groups and was particularly interested in hearing from lesbian and gay people. The session coordinator didn't think such a group would be possible to assemble. She knew of only 1 person in a 3,000-person division who was out. All large organizations have a significant population of lesbians and gays. The number of people who are out is often not an indication of how many lesbians and gays are in the organization. Instead, it often indicates how safe lesbian and gay people feel in the organization and the community.

The solution was simple. The session coordinator told one person— a gay man—about the focus group and that, for safety purposes, it would be held off-site during off-hours so no one's manager or co-workers would wonder why she or he was away for a meeting. The meeting was publicized solely through word of mouth. More than 50 people showed up. With the exception of that one man, none of the 50 felt safe to be out in the organization, but they eagerly embraced the opportunity to share some of their concerns and discuss issues facing lesbian and gay people in the workplace.

In the course of the many Organization R Giving Voice sessions, it was learned that rather than being a culture that leveraged diversity, Organization R's culture publicly prided itself on being blind to differences. People experienced promotion and performance decisions based on favoritism and conformity, not merit. The dominant message was: fit in and don't speak up.

Through the assessment process, Organization R recognized that it had a long way to go to unleash the power of diversity and create an inclusion breakthrough. It also recognized that by undertaking an organizational assessment and conducting Giving Voice sessions, it had made powerful strides in that direction.

One of the hardest elements of the data-gathering process is overcoming skepticism. All too often, people in an organization have lost faith in its willingness or ability to change. Sometimes the first hurdle is assuring people that this time there *is* a commitment to significant change and *everyone* will be required to change, including senior leaders. In this way, the data-gathering process begins getting people on board and positioned for change.

Collecting data is only one step of the assessment process. The most important step is sharing that information with senior executives directly and candidly conveying a vivid picture of peoples' experiences in the organization. Too often, senior executives are sheltered from hearing candid and critical information about what is really going on because no one wants to be the bearer of bad news.

To counter this tendency, a collection of anonymous direct quotes is provided, as well as quantitative data.

Data feedback usually requires a day or day and a half with the executives, and often includes some of their direct reports. At the feedback session, the quantitative and qualitative data are presented, and key findings and specific recommendations for the path forward are made. In most cases, one or more groups of the organization's top performers are included in the assessment process, which makes it clear that the sentiments expressed are not just emanating from the organization's naysayers and malcontents.

BEGIN EDUCATION AND ALIGNMENT

Senior leaders of organizations face significant challenges and opportunities in moving a culture change effort forward. With so much depending on the skills, attitudes, and behaviors modeled by organizational leaders, an inclusion breakthrough effort must include in-depth, multiday educational sessions for senior executives and other leaders in the organization, focusing on leveraging diversity and building inclusion.

Many change efforts fail to gain the total support of the organization because people don't see senior leaders demonstrating the desired new behaviors. People recognize when the senior leaders fail to practice the behaviors and values they are asking of others. This makes the senior leaders' education process critical to an inclusion breakthrough.

Ideally, the education session is a multiday, residential event during which the participants are removed from their everyday work environment. Because leadership education plays a major role in the inclusion breakthrough process, the longer and more intensive the session, the stronger the foundation of the change process.

These days it is a rare to find senior executives and their direct reports who are willing and able to commit multiple days, especially before receiving the data feedback from the organizational assessment. The first step is a two-day session that focuses on the concepts and issues in the data with a more comprehensive educational session held later.

Regardless of its length, the priority of the education session is to provide participants with an understanding of the characteristics and effects of organizational cultures on individual and team performance; the differences between exclusive and inclusive work cultures; the nature and benefits of inclusive behaviors and attitudes, including the importance of using clear and direct communication in all interactions; what it takes to leverage diversity for higher performance; and the nature of strategic culture change.

This session helps senior leaders understand the issues covered in the data feedback session. The education process is essential for positioning the organization's senior leaders to develop action strategies based on what they learn. Usually, as a result of this session, senior leaders are eager to continue their education and commit to additional education to further their learning, understanding, and skills.

Conduct Feedback Sessions with Learning Partners

With much of their time consumed by other organizational responsibilities that keep them from engaging fully with the people of the organization, senior leaders alone cannot carry an entire change effort. To share their vision, responsibility and accountability, the organization's leaders need to engage and partner with a wide range of people in the organization. One such group consists of strategically chosen learning partners. Learning partners should be well respected as important contributors to the organization and represent a diverse cross-section.

In their ordinary routines, senior leaders usually come into contact with a very narrow range of people. When learning partners share their experiences and insights, they enhance the development of senior leaders by providing a broader perspective on such key issues as:

- The current state of the organization

- The challenges ahead

- Their personal experiences in the organization

- The new skills, behaviors and values needed to move the organization forward

- What the learning partners will do to support the senior leaders in moving the organization forward

In addition to helping enrich the senior leaders' educational process, learning partners also help provide leadership to the culture change effort. Not only do they bring the diverse voices of the organization to the senior leaders' attention, they also carry their direct experiences with senior leaders back to the organization as a whole. In this way, they can speak believably and authoritatively about the leaders' vision, commitment, and trustworthiness. As the number of learning partners grows, they help spread the culture change process by building a critical mass of people who practice the new culture's behaviors in their every day work activities.

The benefits of learning partners include the following:

- Provide senior leaders with direct access to voices they might not otherwise hear

- Provide senior leaders with the opportunity for first-hand experience in partnering across a wide range of differences

- Enable senior leaders to exchange ideas and concerns about the change effort and the organization

- Allow senior leaders to begin developing a support system to aid and encourage their development, mentor them, and assist in the implementation of the inclusion breakthrough

- Provide a safe, supportive, yet challenging environment in which senior leaders can practice new behaviors, take risks, and receive honest feedback during and after the educational event

- Broaden the leadership pipeline by acquiring career enhancement skills

- Share their direct experience of different areas in the organization

- Extend leadership of the effort beyond the walls of the executive suite and represent it at all levels of the organization.

Many people from marginalized groups have grown leery of being the "poster child" for differences, trotted out for pictures in the organization's annual report or to prove the organization's commitment to diversity. These people grow weary of helping the organization look good for the world without any real change for them or the organization. It can feel like collusion. Serving as learning partners re-energizes people who may be discouraged about the leaders' commitment and sincerity about change. They leave the session energized and recommitted to being ambassadors and informal leaders of the initiative. They also benefit by the broader contact with senior leaders, which promotes greater visibility and upward mobility.

After the data feedback session in one organization, its senior leaders were disturbed by what the data indicated: People believed that promotions were based on favoritism, women were harassed and were not allowed adequate maternity leave benefits, and people of color were seen as being too risky to promote. At an educational retreat held for senior executives, the learning partners who had been selected from among the organization's highest performers spoke honestly about their experiences, verifying the feedback data. As a result of the session, the CEO changed the maternity benefits the very next day. The CEO assigned a senior vice president to co-chair a Diversity and Inclusion Action Task Force to address the other issues and opportunities raised and issued an organization-wide statement, communicating to the entire workforce why an inclusion breakthrough was critical to their success.

After the third year of its inclusion breakthrough effort, the organization had developed a reputation as one of the best places for women to work and a place in which promotions were based on honest and fair evaluations.

In another organization, several individuals were flouting recently established harassment policies by circulating racist jokes on the organization's intranet system. Making a strong statement in support of the organization's Zero Tolerance for Harassment policy, the CEO ordered that the individuals be fired on the spot and escorted from the building.

The results of leadership education and data feedback sessions at one long-established Fortune 100 company generated the following actions to help build the platform for change: (1) an organization-wide forum was held, focusing on building inclusion and leveraging diversity, chaired by the CEO; (2) a new department and new positions were created and funded specifically related to achieving higher performance by building inclusion and leveraging diversity; and (3) a personal letter, signed by the CEO, was sent to each member of the organization, explaining the change process and the business reasons for it.

As isolated efforts, these actions would not have had a lasting effect. But as the kick-off for a long-term process, each was highly effective. Now, more than a year later, virtually all members of the organization have a thorough knowledge of the 11 Inclusive Behaviors and are evaluated continuously on their ability to demonstrate them.

IDENTIFY INTERNAL LEADERSHIP FOR THE CHANGE EFFORT

Leaders often underestimate the effects of their behavior on the behavior and performance of the people in their organizations.

Some think they can simply legislate new behavior patterns by announcing a new set of policies and rules. And many are surprised when the people of the organization emulate their leadership style instead of adhering to their words and announced policies.

Senior leaders alone cannot create an effective inclusion breakthrough. They must extend their leadership to others in the organization who can partner with them and support the effort, bringing their diverse skills, talents, and perspectives to its successful implementation. They must empower others as leaders and then be prepared to follow *their* lead.

As a symbolic action, this demonstrates commitment to the culture change and belief in the values of the new culture. As a practical action, it creates an expanded leadership group with the broad vision and variety of perspectives needed to plan and implement a far-reaching, long-range effort.

To reach these goals, the change effort's leadership team must be both diverse and inclusive. That means people from the organization's dominant culture—usually the culture of the founders—must be represented, as well as people from other groups. If a diversity effort's leadership team is comprised exclusively of people whose social identity would be seen as representing the newer groups, it runs the danger of being perceived by the majority of the organization as a group of "them," severely hampering its credibility and effectiveness. This type of team also is not truly inclusive. Many diversity task forces are limited in their diversity.

The goal of this leadership team is to assist in the development and implementation of actions that will benefit the entire organization. As such, it must represent the entire organization and be able to speak credibly for it.

How the group is selected is important. In one organization, where hierarchy and chain of command were critical, it was essential that the initial action team be made up of high-level individuals, including one of the co-chairs being a member of the executive committee. In other organizations, where there is greater experience and opportunity for cross-functional teams, it makes more sense to create an action team that incorporates all levels.

At Organization S, a major business-services organization that made a strong commitment to achieving an inclusion breakthrough, a great deal of care went into selecting and developing a leadership team to guide, manage, and champion the effort.

The Inclusion Implementation Work Team included three people from the highest level of Organization S, and it reported directly to the CEO. There were three co-chairs of this team: one of the most senior executives, a white man; a high-level manager, an African American man; and another high-level manager, a white woman.

The team was responsible for ensuring that the organization addressed issues of achieving higher performance, building inclusion and leveraging diversity in its policies, practices, behaviors and resource allocations. Its tasks included the following:

- Advising the CEO on all matters relating to building inclusion, leveraging diversity, and enabling people to do their best work

- Assisting the senior executives to develop, implement and sustain a long-term culture change effort

- Developing and communicating the organizational imperative for an inclusion breakthrough

- Monitoring the alignment of policies, practices, and behaviors across the organization with the inclusion breakthrough strategies and goals

- Modeling the values and behaviors of the new culture and their effectiveness in enabling high performance

TAKE ACTION IN AREAS THAT NEED ATTENTION

Early in the change process is the critical time for actions that are both substantive and symbolic. People will be wondering what came out of the data-collection and assessment process. Was this just another exercise or are the organization's leaders truly committed to change? To build a platform for change, it is imperative that the findings and the path forward are communicated to the organization and that a bold public statement is made, demonstrating that the change process is real and that the very top of the organization is committed to it.

Examples of this kind of action might be establishing a new senior-level position responsible for supporting and monitoring the organization's efforts in leveraging diversity and inclusion; enacting a new, more inclusive professional development policy; or the dismissal or reassignment of a manager known for discriminatory behaviors.

SUMMARY OF PHASE I STRATEGIES

The purpose of phase I is to develop a solid foundation for change. This is accomplished by assessing how successfully the organization has positioned the effort as a way of life—establishing the organizational imperative for the change effort; undertaking a comprehensive organizational assessment that includes both a written survey and focus groups; conducting education and data feedback sessions; taking immediate actions for change; and identifying and developing internal leaders who will partner with senior leaders.

All of these steps are critical elements to ready the organization for change but should not be confused with the change itself. These steps are analogous to tilling the soil, cultivating the field, and preparing it to receive the seeds of change.

Chapter

9

Creating Momentum

Phase I of mobilizing for an inclusion breakthrough focuses on identifying, developing and aligning resources and positioning the effort for implementation. As the more action-oriented phase II gets under way (see Table 6), it is important to create momentum in the organization by emphasizing the mission critical nature of the process.

This is the time to make clear to everyone in the organization that life is going to change. Leaders of the effort must be prepared to be more visible. They must be ready to model the competencies and behaviors that they want to encourage in others and be prepared for the feedback, verbal and nonverbal, given to all pioneers of change. There will be new expectations, required competencies, and ways of behaving and working together.

DEVELOP INITIAL SHORT-TERM PLAN

In developing the initial 12-to-18-month plan for implementing organization-wide culture change, the inclusion breakthrough leadership team should focus on building and sustaining momentum to make it happen. The elements of phase II should be incorporated into the plan, including the strategies and actions that emerged from the data feedback process.

Table 6: Phase II of the KJCG methodology for an inclusion breakthrough

PHASE II: CREATING MOMENTUM			
• Develop initial 12- to 18-month plan	• Implement aggressive efforts to engage, inform and enroll the people of the organization • Develop a critical mass of Agents of Change	• Begin education to create new competencies for senior leaders, managers, individual contributors • Create processes to address blatant or subtle discrimination/ barriers	• Support networks, mentoring, coaching and buddy systems • Identify and begin work in "Pockets of Readiness"

IMPLEMENT AGGRESSIVE EFFORTS TO ENGAGE, INFORM, AND ENROLL

As the inclusion breakthrough begins gathering momentum, the need to create realistic expectations also escalates. Aggressive, active communications ensure that everyone in the organization is well informed of the initiative's goals, plans and rationale.

There should be frequent and various communications from the senior executives of the organization regarding the details, expectations and the anticipated benefits of the change effort. It is important to sustain the momentum in the organization by emphasizing the importance of the process and the organizational imperative for the inclusion breakthrough.

DEVELOP A CRITICAL MASS OF AGENTS OF CULTURE CHANGE

To help build a critical mass of people who are actively living the new culture and practicing inclusive behaviors in their work, a core group (from 50 to 400, depending on the size of the organization) of agents of culture change should be selected for intensive education and skill-development training. They will become role models and experts in the behaviors and business rationale for the new culture, to seed the organization with informal leaders who will demonstrate the new culture's behaviors and values in their day-to-day interactions. This initial group will select change partners (peers or managers) to participate in some of the educational events, which will expand the group further.

At Organization T, rolling out an organization-wide inclusion effort was particularly challenging because the organization had many different divisions, business units, and work sites. The initial 18-month plan developed by its Inclusion Implementation Work Team met this challenge by adopting the following approaches:

- **Leadership and communication from the top:** The CEO of Organization T sent a personalized letter to the home of every employee, articulating the organizational imperative for building inclusion and leveraging diversity and the organization's commitment to creating a culture of inclusion. The letter discussed the findings from the organizational assessment and outlined the plans to change the organization's culture. The organization's monthly newsletter followed up with a series of articles about the change effort, further positioning it as a visible, high-priority effort being supported at all levels of the organization. The monthly articles also continued to connect the inclusion breakthrough effort to the organization's business strategies and direction.

- **Organization-wide Action Group:** This sub-group of the Inclusion Implementation Work Team was established to provide visible, accountable leadership for the inclusion breakthrough process. The CEO's visible support for the Work Team lent additional credence to the seriousness of the effort. The group's first step was to identify inclusion-oriented policies, practices and behaviors that needed to be integrated into business plans and strategies at all levels of the organization.

- **Organization-wide Feedback:** To align the entire organization and drive change throughout the divisions, data feedback sessions were conducted with division leaders and learning partners to make sure that the information gathered by the organizational assessment was fully understood as it applied to each division and local work unit. This became the starting point from which the divisions developed their own Divisional Inclusion Councils, designed to integrate the culture change effort in their particular organizations.

- **Integrating the culture change into divisional business plans:** The Divisional Inclusion Councils partnered with their unit leaders to develop specific strategic business plans that would empower people in their division to integrate the effort to achieve high performance, build inclusion, and leverage diversity into their day-to-day and long-term practices. The Divisional Inclusion Councils also worked closely with the Inclusion Implementation Work Team to ensure alignment and avoid duplication of efforts.

- **Vice president, Office of Organizational Performance and Inclusion:** A new position was created, providing a full-time, dedicated internal resource to oversee and drive the change process. Reporting directly to the CEO, this function (with staff) partnered with such internal change groups as the Inclusion Implementation Work Team and the Divisional Inclusion Councils, senior leaders, external consultants, and all division-level and local-level operations involved in the inclusion breakthrough.

- **Organization-wide orientation sessions:** The Inclusion Implementation Work Team developed a four-hour orientation and enrollment program that was rolled out to all members of the organization. In these sessions, senior leaders partnering with members of the Work Team explained the inclusion breakthrough effort and introduced the new behaviors that were now expected of everyone. In a three-month period, all 4000 members of the organization had spent at least a half-day learning what the inclusion breakthrough was all about, why it was important to the business and the new expectations of behaviors to support the effort. In these forums, members of the organization were able to ask questions and get answers from the senior leaders about how the change effort would affect the business and their work experience.

- **Human resources education:** To prepare for the increased emphasis on integrating and aligning people-centric policies and procedures with the organization's operations, several educational workshops were held for the human resources staff. Topics included understanding the organizational imperative, modeling this understanding as a function of their duties, and applying it at the policy level and in day-to-day activities. The goal was to strengthen the capabilities and perspectives in the human resources department so it could more effectively partner with line managers in this process—not to have the effort owned by human resources, but to empower the staff to serve as partners and resources to others involved in the inclusion breakthrough effort.

- **Agents of Culture Change education series:** Groups of 50 people were selected to serve as agents of culture change. The groups were diverse with regard to social identity, function, and level. The agents of culture change became a high-performing, diverse, and inclusive community from which each member could draw strength and support for their efforts. These groups of 50 agents each received 18 days of education about change and building inclusion and leveraging diversity for higher performance. When they completed their education, the agents of culture change were responsible for being role models and bringing a new lens to their day-to-day business interactions. During their education, each agent of culture change selected two change partners to join them for three days of the educational series, which created a support base and extended the learning to others. After the first Agents of Culture Change series, two additional groups were selected and educated during the first 18 months of the effort. In this way, a critical mass of 450 people (150 agents of culture change and 300 change partners) were incorporated into the process.

EDUCATE TO CREATE NEW COMPETENCIES

Despite any number of diversity awareness programs, executive memos, vision statements and corporate directives, the inclusiveness of a work environment is most strongly affected by the immediate manager. Culture change does not become visible, viable, and believable until managers and leaders at all levels embrace and model the change.

The education of managers is a critical component of creating a new set of competencies in the organization. Managers' influence on the experiences of the people they manage is great. The old saying is true: If they're not part of the solution, they're part of the problem.

Managers and leaders at all levels must be able to translate the organization's business and operational needs for leveraging diversity and inclusion into everyday practice. For many managers, this requires a new mindset that allows them to see the connection between managing people and achieving organizational results. It also requires new skills for communicating, partnering, coaching, and building inclusion.

Managers can be one of the resistance points in a culture change effort. Many midlevel managers, for instance, have spent their entire careers living, breathing, and succeeding in the old culture. But, although they were seen as highly competent in the old culture, they may lack the skills to lead or succeed in the new culture.

Five days of specialized education for all managers, in the form of two separate multiday sessions with groups of managers from different levels and areas of an organization, is recommended.

Three consecutive full days is the minimum time required for an effective first session. For subsequent sessions, multiple-day events are recommended because of the time required to establish a viable "learning community" (KJCG, 1997, 1998) in each session.

This kind of manager education is an essential part of an initial plan for achieving an inclusion breakthrough, but it should also be viewed as a temporary, emergency intervention. For the long run, the skills needed for leveraging diversity and building inclusion must be integrated into all formal and informal leadership and management education processes and on-the-job training that takes place between each person and her or his manager. If learning and using these skills is kept separate from the business practices and not mainstreamed, they will be regarded as optional, inessential, and disconnected from everyday operations and organizational goals.

A Managing for High Performance and Inclusion education program is now under way at several companies. The program improves a manager's ability to create and lead a more inclusive workgroup; to increase her or his self-awareness and knowledge of leveraging diversity issues; to encourage change; to communicate more effectively across differences; to resolve conflict and disagreements more effectively; and to leverage the diversity of the work group for better decision-making and problem solving.

The first three-day manager education session provides increased understanding and skills. Although senior leaders and managers begin to get an initial understanding of other peoples' key issues and experiences during phase I of the change effort, to be effective as leaders they need to further develop their competencies and abilities.

The second part of the managers' education program is a two-day practicum. During this segment, managers bring in three or four members of their staff. Together they learn and practice vital skills by addressing and accepting conflict as a byproduct of the synergy produced by diversity, solving problems and giving honest and candid feedback across differences. After the practicum, the managers and teams go back and train their team members. Teaching others reinforces their learning while expanding the knowledge base throughout the organization.

Through this education and training, managers develop a shared perspective for leveraging diversity and inclusion; enhanced skills and competence in leading and managing a diverse workforce; and the tools needed to support an inclusion breakthrough.

CREATE PROCESSES TO ADDRESS DISCRIMINATION

One major aspect of moving toward an inclusion breakthrough is eliminating any barriers that might cause discrimination. Addressing these barriers signals to the people of the organization the seriousness of the effort and the commitment to change. Barriers such as hidden differentials in salaries between women and men, lagging promotions for people of color, and structural and physical barriers that limit access for people with disabilities all need to be addressed.

Several organizations involved in inclusion breakthrough efforts have established Inclusion Action Teams that meet regularly to identify such barriers to inclusion and discuss solutions. In most cases, these teams have found that some barriers must be identified and addressed before other, more subtle barriers are even noticed.

The experience of Organization U is an example of the progressive nature of this kind of work. During a meeting with the Workplace Culture Team, the organization's senior executives learned that lack of domestic partner benefits was a barrier to lesbian and gay members. Charged with developing a domestic partner benefits policy for the worldwide organization, the Workplace Culture Team soon realized that a whole realm of policies targeted to heterosexual married people were not being extended to the organization's lesbian and gay members. The team was able to implement a number of improvements that resulted in substantial gains in the organization's capability to recruit and retain lesbian and gay people.

SUPPORT NETWORKS, BUDDY SYSTEMS, AND COACHING

Many for-profit companies and nonprofit organizations now sponsor the formation of networks (also called affinity groups) for various demographic groups, with mixed results. Several organizations established networks for underrepresented populations as part of diversity awareness initiatives. While helping to foster connections and alleviate feelings of isolation, these efforts also tended to produce friction, because others perceived them as efforts to serve and respond to specific groups' demands without any real connection to business outcomes. They also engendered frustration in their members because these networks were usually under funded and denied significant input into business decisions. People outside these identified groups often viewed the networks with suspicion, and some people who were of the identified groups viewed them with scorn. As one person said, "I've been working here for 15 years. I don't need any support group. I'm doing just fine, thank you."

In other organizations, stiff competition for workforce talent leads to the creation of network groups as part of a recruitment and retention strategy. These groups, especially those having the active involvement of senior executives, produce positive results. Indeed, their active support was one of the organization's critical success factors for career development by attracting top talent and reducing turnover. This is particularly true among members of traditionally underrepresented and unsupported groups.

For example, Organization V linked its networks inextricably with the organization's bottom-line objectives.

As part of an organization-wide culture change effort to improve performance through building inclusion and leveraging diversity, the organization's leadership actively supported the formation of networks, with several key provisos:

- As part of its charter, each network must identify its connection to the organization's business objectives and outline the ways in which its actions contribute to the success of the organization's mission.

- Each network has a senior leader as its champion. In practice, these champions are usually not of the networks' primary identity groups. They provide a sounding board for network action proposals and a senior-level advocate for the network's projects and points of view.

- Each network belongs to the overall network of networks. A group, consisting of leaders of each network, meets regularly to keep the groups focused and aligned on business objectives and plans joint activities that connect the organization with the community.

After only two years of implementation, Organization V found the business benefits of the networks to be significant. The Latino Network was a key resource for recruiting talent and developing new customers from Latino/Latina communities. This group was also active in screening candidates with Spanish-speaking capabilities and serving as a resource for hiring managers.

The People of Color and Gay-Lesbian networks provided unprecedented coaching and development for their members. As a result, they have succeeded in developing business relationships with people of their social identity groups and transforming the organization's products to meet the needs of those communities.

Alignment with the organization's bottom line is a key success factor for the networks. The ability to contribute to the success of the organization through this kind of network activity lends credibility and a sense of value to the network members.

One woman said that without the efforts of these networks, she would have left the organization three years ago. Since then, she has brought in $600,000 of new business in less than a year. That is the kind of bottom-line benefit that organizations love to support.

In some organizations, however, the lack of networking opportunities for white men has contributed to perceptions of reverse discrimination.

Despite the common belief that white men already have their network—the good old boys—white men need networks too. They need a place to feel safe to learn about being partners and allies with members of all social identity groups and other networks that are working to build the organization's inclusive culture. A white men's network is an important part of enabling white men to understand the true meaning of inclusion and is a base from which they can reach out to other white men to help facilitate positive change.

Two ways to extend the envelope of inclusion to an organization's new people are establishing buddy systems and training managers to become partners in the development of their new hires.

A buddy system is an extended orientation process that assigns each new hire a buddy who is an established, high-performing member of the new hire's workgroup. The buddy is responsible for showing the new hire the ropes and helping her or him succeed in the organization. The key to making this process work is to hold both the buddy and the workgroup's manager accountable for the success of the new hire throughout the first year of her or his employment. One effective way to accomplish this is to tie bonus compensation for both the manager and the buddy to the retention, productivity, and progress of the new hire. In this way, all new hires have at least two highly motivated allies they can look to for support and guidance. Some organizations are also establishing buddies when people transfer to new divisions, recognizing that different parts of the organization may have different approaches and unwritten rules for success.

Managers need to be coaches, mentors, facilitators, and partners, not just scorekeepers and attendance takers. Coaching and mentoring need to be formal, measured parts of their job descriptions and accountabilities, with performance reflected in their compensation.

IDENTIFY AND LEVERAGE
POCKETS OF READINESS

Senior leaders think that to implement change in large organizations, the entire organization must move ahead together. Inevitably, certain business units or functions can move a lot faster than the rest of the organization. These pockets of readiness can be advantageous to the change effort because they can model the change, create new definitions of success, and demonstrate the benefits of the effort for the rest of the organization.

A mistake made during many change efforts is an excessive focus of available energy and resources on the areas most resistant to change—a strategy analogous to attempting to storm a castle by attacking the most heavily defended parapet. It is far more practical and effective to start with the people and business units most willing to move forward and demonstrate success through practicing new, more inclusive behaviors and skills.

After an organization has a successful unit to hold up as a model, ongoing success is more likely because people can see that not only does an inclusion breakthrough work, it works better. People who see the success of this higher performing group will say, "We want to be like them. We want to do what they are doing."

Then, instead of the organization being *pushed* toward leveraging diversity and a culture of inclusion, it starts to *pull* itself forward along the path. Pushing creates resistance. Success lies in getting people to see the value of the change so that they want to move toward it.

SUMMARY OF PHASE II STRATEGIES

A change effort of this scale requires a great many actions, all of which seem critical, but not all of which are immediately practical or possible. Budgets and the availability of resources must be established. Priorities must be determined. If the organization does not change, it may eventually perish—but if it does not continue to conduct its day-to-day business, it certainly will perish.

Therefore, the following priorities in planning and implementing the initial 12-to-18-month strategy of phase II are recommended: First, develop resources, policies, and competencies that will support the inclusion breakthrough in the long term. Second, connect the inclusion breakthrough to the bottom-line objectives and mission of the organization. In implementing both of these priorities, there should be another, overriding priority: Pursue the inclusion breakthrough in a manner that reflects and models the competencies and ways of doing business it is intended to create.

Making Diversity and Inclusion a Way of Life

After the organization has built a platform for change and created momentum for the change effort, the leaders of the inclusion breakthrough are positioned to apply what they have learned about leveraging diversity, building inclusion and strategic culture change to accomplish goals they could not have defined before embarking on the effort.

Key to developing an expanded and longer-term plan for achieving and sustaining the inclusion breakthrough is leveraging the new competencies, resources, and organizational capabilities that have been gained since phase I (see Table 7). They make a new realm of strategies possible. Even more significantly, they make a new realm of strategies *doable*.

DEVELOP A LONG-TERM STRATEGIC PLAN

The inclusion breakthrough must be an integral part of how the organization does business, gains and maintains its competitive position, pursues profitability and plans its future. The culture change must be part of the overall master plan of the organization, not simply its diversity plan or people utilization plan.

Central to this phase of the change process is developing strategies that link the inclusion breakthrough to all of the organization's

Table 7: Phase III of the KJG methodology for an inclusion breakthrough

PHASE III: MAKING DIVERSITY AND INCLUSION A WAY OF LIFE			
• Expand the initial plan to a long-term strategic plan that integrates and partners with all change initiatives	• Formalize accountability for living the competencies in the new culture (scorecards & other tools) • Baseline diversity and inclusion into all education, training and programs	• Implement incentives and rewards to support the Inclusion Breakthrough and to create organizational pull • Enhance performance feedback systems to support the new culture	• Involve stakeholders (e.g., suppliers, joint ventures, acquisitions, community, board members)

operations and process-improvement initiatives. Such strategies include applying inclusion-oriented competencies to achieve breakthrough transformations in customer service, product design, and market-development planning. The starting point may be a culture change effort, but the results include a repositioning of the organization's products and services for a more sustainable future.

At this point, leaders at all levels of the organization have participated in phase I and phase II education sessions. They have gained an understanding of the activities and resources needed to foster an inclusion breakthrough, as well as the requisite skills. A core group of agents for culture change has been developed. Members of this group are valuable assets in planning and implementing the strategies needed to integrate the inclusion breakthrough in all aspects of the business.

Although it would be possible to establish the elements and actions of an expanded effort immediately following the organizational assessment, doing so would likely undermine the effort's success. The understanding gained during education will shape how strategies are devised and implemented in ways that cannot be anticipated before experiencing the education process.

Organization W had worked diligently for almost two years at laying the foundation for its inclusion breakthrough strategy. The organization had created an inclusion breakthrough leadership team selected from its organizational leaders, high potentials and learning partners, all of whom had received a significant amount of education and training related to leveraging diversity and building inclusion.

Striving for 360-degree vision, the team comprised itself of people from all levels of the organization and created a diverse group in terms of gender, race, age and ethnicity. Most of the members had been involved in the work of phase I and phase II. Some had been part of the initial Giving Voice focus groups, and others had completed Agents for Culture Change education. Some were managers, some were senior leaders, a few were new hires, and others were considered thought leaders in their areas.

To further institutionalize the new culture, the Inclusion Breakthrough Leadership Team worked with each division to assess behavioral change at the individual, divisional, and corporate levels. An annual employee survey, Diversity and Inclusion Index, was developed to explicitly measure peoples' perceptions of progress.

The Diversity and Inclusion Index was a baseline measure to assess improvement with respect to perceptions of leveraging diversity and a culture of inclusion—specific measures related to the extent to which people experience a sense of belonging and are able to speak up and practice skills of inclusion. After the baseline was established, it was used to monitor progress on an annual basis of the organizational environment and became a part of performance measures and accountability. Organization W was able to link compensation to acquiring and living the new competencies. They were also better positioned to plan and guide all aspects of the improvement process—coaching, skill building, education, and communication.

A balanced scorecard that measured both financial performance and performance with respect to people and culture was established.

This enabled the organization to be accountable for its progress and to announce inclusion breakthrough milestones in its public statements and reports to stakeholders. At the individual level, demonstration of inclusive behaviors was incorporated as a critical success factor in a new performance measure. At the divisional and corporate levels, human resources tracked the success of the organization in attracting, retaining, developing, and promoting a diverse talent base through the Leveraging Diversity and Inclusion Improvement Metrics. The Improvement Metrics included workforce composition—new hires, promotion, turnover rates, and grade levels—succession planning, audit composition and performance management.

Divisional and corporate scorecards focused on successes related to retention and development of a diverse talent pool as well as business relationships with suppliers, distributors, and customers that increased the overall diversity of these groups.

Leaders were required to identify the specific inclusive behaviors on which to base their evaluation. They received comprehensive feedback from their peers, managers, and direct reports. Their success in practicing the behaviors was tied to their compensation and bonus.

Advanced strategies like these maintained the organization's focus for the long haul. The initial plan must be expanded to become part of the organization's strategic planning processes to ensure that all change and business initiatives are integrated.

FORMALIZE ACCOUNTABILITY

What is measured is what gets accomplished. The key to sustainable success for organizations that want long-term change is the development of effective measurements for the new behaviors and the capability to hold people accountable for using them. This will require new tools for measuring individual and group behaviors as well as results related to inclusion and leveraging diversity, such as a

Diversity and Inclusion Index and Leveraging Diversity and Inclusion Improvement Metrics.

Managers must play a major role in the change effort, both in modeling the new behaviors and in holding people accountable for practicing them. Managers have the second-biggest influence on whether people stay or leave (their immediate work team has the biggest influence). Managers are seen as the most important source of training and mentoring, as well as the primary gatekeepers to raises, bonuses, flextime, dependent-care benefits, opportunities, career development, and advancement.

BASELINE LEVERAGING DIVERSITY EDUCATION

As people begin seeing through their new inclusion-oriented lenses and diversity and inclusion become more and more a way of life in the organization, the need to communicate a consistent message becomes critical. Education and training related to diversity and inclusion must move from being one-off activities that have their own special place isolated from the mainstream, to being fully integrated into all education and training.

The leadership must identify the new skills that the organization needs to succeed. Requirements for these skills will then be reflected in all people-development processes, including retention, recruitment, and technical training programs.

Such skills include the ability to communicate and partner across differences and contribute effectively to inclusive teams. The organization must reassess what it looks for in new hires, how it conducts training programs, and how its leadership-development process can emphasize these new skills.

As discussed in phase II, much of the early intensive education is designed to jump-start the effort. Education that raises an individual's awareness and develops shared perceptions about the need for a more diverse workforce is essential in the early phases of an inclusion breakthrough. In addition, intensive education for managers is essential so that they can learn the new skills and competencies to lead and leverage a diverse workforce and create an inclusive environment. In phase III, the messages and skills must become integrated into all aspects of the organization's training and education—from new manager training to sales training, from interviewing skills to coaching and mentoring courses. Diversity and inclusion concepts, skills, and processes must be integrated in course content, staffing, and delivery. In this way, diversity becomes part of the baseline education, with little need for stand-alone, one-off training or education.

IMPLEMENT INCENTIVES

It may sound like an oversimplification, but people tend to do what they are to paid to do. In other words, people tend to practice and repeat behaviors for which they are rewarded. Providing financial incentives for behaviors and accomplishments that support the culture change effort is a time-proven strategy.

Organizations that position inclusive practices as simply the right thing to do often expect people to change long-established behaviors with only a moral incentive. This can place people in the no-win position of having to choose between (a) discouraged actions that feel comfortable and carry no penalty and (b) encouraged actions that feel uncomfortable and sometimes awkward and carry no reward.

Effective rewards and incentives for individuals include bonuses for living the behaviors learned in education sessions; measurable success in mentoring, coaching, or buddying (success could be defined by retention, promotion, or job satisfaction); being "caught" doing something right by colleagues; or integrating inclusive practices and strategies into formal business plans within specified time limits.

Effective rewards and incentives for teams, workgroups and business units include group or unit bonuses for achieving retention aspirations or other culture-measurement goals.

ENHANCE PERFORMANCE FEEDBACK SYSTEMS

Throughout the entire inclusion breakthrough strategy, attention must be paid to aligning management policies, practices, and procedures. In phase III it is critical that performance feedback and management mechanisms align with the inclusion breakthrough and fully support the new behaviors now expected of each member of the organization.

For example, manager performance should be evaluated by those who report to them and their peers to make sure that managers' behaviors align with the policies and performance objectives and the values of the organization.

INVOLVE STAKEHOLDERS

Communicating business gains to the organization's stakeholders is a key to enlisting their support for institutionalizing change. Demonstrating and utilizing inclusive practices when interacting with suppliers and distributors—treating them like partners and not vendors—helps develop more productive relationships. Developing and building on these partnerships is an ongoing part of inclusion breakthrough, requiring expanded levels of respect, inclusion and mutuality in interactions. For example, some organizations require suppliers to sign agreements ensuring that there will be no harassment, they will increase their diversity, and they will pay people a living wage. Some organizations begin to rethink who their key stakeholders are and expand the reach to include a more diverse supplier base.

PUT PLANNING INTO ACTION

Phase III of the methodology is about integrating the behaviors, policies, and strategies of the inclusion breakthrough into all aspects of organizational life. By expanding the initial culture change plan into a long-range strategic plan, the organization is making a formal commitment to the change process. It is clearly not a flavor of the month.

Establishing accountability systems, incentives, and rewards for supporting the new culture will help motivate people to learn and practice the new behaviors. Making the inclusion breakthrough an integral part of ongoing change initiatives, education, and training ensures that the skills and strategies for leveraging diversity and building inclusion will become and remain standard operating procedure. An organization can make plans upon plans but if they don't execute them, it is just a lot of wasted paper. Organizations need to put their planning into action.

Organization X faced the classic mature-market manufacturing dilemma: How can you increase profits without increasing prices when you already own the lion's share of the market?

The obvious answer was to reduce costs. That meant streamlining manufacturing processes and business practices that had kept Organization X a world leader for more than a century. It also meant reducing headcount. But Organization X found that cutting its payroll had unexpected costs. Worker morale plummeted and teamwork suffered as people saw their friends forced to leave and viewed their teammates as competitors for the dwindling number of jobs. Innovation dried up as downsizing-related fears prevented people from trying new approaches or voicing new ideas. Trust in management eroded as people blamed their leaders for the loss of jobs that had supported some families for generations.

Employee surveys and cultural assessments conducted over the previous decade had painted a consistent picture of everyday life in Organization X. The areas of challenge and conflict were clear:

- Command-and-control hierarchy

- Need-to-know basis for communications

- Who-you-know criteria for advancement

- Divide-and-conquer divisional segregation

- Mechanistic model of humans as interchangeable cogs

- Downward-only flow of information and accountability

- Focus on layoffs and reducing expenditure

- Avoidance of risk-taking and suppression of innovation

Over the previous ten years, consulting firms had recommended various programs that had been implemented through management initiatives. It seemed that no one from the shop floor to the executive suite expected any of these programs to have any lasting or useful effect.

In starting a new culture change effort aimed at creating an inclusion breakthrough, it became clear that one of the greatest difficulties in rallying support for the effort would be overcoming pessimism and making diversity and inclusion a way of life.

To begin designing a change process that would address Organization X's culture, as well as its current and future business needs, the first priority was to establish internal ownership and stewardship of the change effort. To gain buy-in from people at all levels of the organization, volunteers from across the organization were invited to join in forming a cross-functional and multilevel Partnering for Change Team. For many people, this was the first opportunity to speak and partner with others outside their own work groups.

During the culture-assessment interviews conducted at the beginning of the new effort, interviewers identified a cadre of promising candidates for this team. These candidates and others who appeared committed to positive change were invited to join the change process. The Partnering for Change Team was diverse in terms of gender, race, age, and length of service, as well as in job function and hierarchical level.

Before beginning the planning process, the Partnering for Change Team had three days of intensive education on the topics of leveraging diversity, building inclusion, high performance, and strategic culture change. The Team's education also included an in-depth review of the cultural-assessment and employee survey findings. After identifying specific areas of opportunity, the Partnering for Change Team formed action teams and developed detailed, bottom-line-oriented recommendations, which they presented to Organization X's senior leadership team for approval.

The result was a comprehensive set of organizational behaviors and change strategies that worked together to create and support a new culture and new way of doing business. Implemented more than a year ago, the strategies are now in full swing and are beginning to show dramatic results. The key strategies include the following:

- **Spreading the word:** Sharing the vision of a new culture change

- **Leading change:** Educating managers and leaders

- **Sending downsizing up:** Accelerating culture change through leadership reorganization

- **Subverting the old culture:** Building a critical mass of internal change agents

Sharing the vision of a new culture
The Partnering for Change Team developed one-day education sessions for the entire population of Organization X. Presented daily to groups of 100 Organization X members at a time, the sessions provided an overview of the planned change process, as well as

interactive discussions about ways in which the change would affect people's work lives. The sessions also delineated specific behavioral expectations and provided instruction in the 11 Inclusive Behaviors (described in chapter 3). People walked out of the sessions knowing what was coming; what was expected of them; and how to create a more inclusive environment in their work lives and personal lives.

Educating managers and leaders

Based on recommendations from the Partnering for Change Team, all managers and team leaders were required to attend a three-day education session on issues of leveraging diversity, building inclusion, higher performance, and change.

Accelerating culture change through leadership reorganization

To address the issue of leadership competence, the Partnering for Change Team created a new profile of desired competencies for leaders and managers, a methodology for evaluating the qualifications of current managers and prospective management candidates, and a competency-based leadership-development process. The key changes were adding people-skills to the portfolio of required leadership competencies, and creating a procedure for evaluating and reassigning leaders and managers based on those required competencies.

Building a critical mass of internal change agents

One of the hardest parts of leveraging diversity and creating a culture of inclusion is finding credible models for people to follow. Few people have been part of a group that encourages and leverages differences of culture, style, experience, and point of view of every person in the group or team. Few people are ready to believe that differences and working to include each person are not barriers to higher performance, but necessary for highest performance.

Based on the recommendations of the Partnering for Change Team, Organization X committed significant resources to select, educate, and support ten groups of agents of culture change. These groups created among themselves a culture of inclusion and were then able to carry out their mission: to take the knowledge and skills to their day-to-day work interactions and processes.

The changes in attitude and environment were visible throughout Organization X. As a result of the leadership competence and assessment process, approximately 25 percent of the managers were reassigned to non-managerial duties and another 30 percent were placed on probation with a requirement to start living the new values and behaviors through demonstrated and measured action in the next four to six months. Those who did not acquire and practice the required competencies within the timeframe were reassigned or asked to leave.

Ongoing survey results showed that people feel more than twice as favorably toward their managers and leaders as they did just two years ago. Strongly favorable responses about people's future with the organization have increased by more than 50 percent. More people were planning longer commitments to their jobs and to the organization's future.

Perhaps more dramatic still were the changes in the ways that people greeted and meet one another within Organization X work areas. Thanks to a strong upsurge of inclusive behaviors, more people said hello to one another and included more voices and faces in their conversations and activities. Workgroup meetings enjoyed greater participation, and more people took part in decision-making processes. People actively sought out the opinions of previously overlooked colleagues. Managers were sought out and engaged as coaches and mentors instead of mistrusted and avoided. And new ideas were raised, supported, and shared up, down, and across the organization.

For Organization X, the inclusion breakthrough was not just a new flavor; it was truly a new beginning.

SUMMARY OF PHASE III STRATEGIES

By the time all phase III strategies have been implemented, the inclusion breakthrough will be felt in all corners and corridors of the organization. Except for isolated pockets of resistance, leveraging diversity and building inclusion will be the everyday way of operating throughout the organization. The new competencies might not be flawless or totally graceful, but they will be practiced or at least aspired to in virtually all workplace and external interactions. The new sense of energy, purpose, and community will be pervasive and unmistakable. Visitors and newcomers to the organization will feel it in the air.

Leveraging Learning and Challenging the New Status Quo

Phase IV of the methodology to achieve an inclusion breakthrough might be described as "Going Forward Back to Phase I." To sustain the inclusion breakthrough, it must be continually recreated (see Table 8). Even a highly diverse group can grow static and overly comfortable with the new status quo unless it constantly strives to increase and leverage its diversity and expand its parameters of inclusion.

Just as the strategies of phase III cannot be formed or implemented until the lessons of phases I and II have been experienced and learned, the strategies of phase IV use what has been learned from the first three phases to evaluate the progress to date and reassess the needs of the organization in light of the changes in perspective and circumstance since the start of the inclusion breakthrough.

Another key to the success of the inclusion breakthrough is the understanding that unforeseen issues will arise. The organization's senior leaders must build in the flexibility to deal with these unexpected issues as they arise.

REASSESS PROGRESS AND GAPS

In addition to measurements of performance and progress, another way to assess whether the process is meeting objectives is through

Table 8: Phase IV of the KJCG methodology for an inclusion breakthrough

PHASE IV: LEVERAGING LEARNING AND CHALLENGING THE NEW STATUS QUO			
• Reassess organization to identify progress and gaps • Reassess how the work of the organization is done	• Communicate accomplishments and success practices internally and externally	• Identify and address areas that will support higher and higher performance	• Continuously improve the change process

periodic re-surveys and comparisons. Although the effort should be viewed as a commitment to continuous improvement, the structures of the effort should not be viewed as intractable or permanent.

The inclusion breakthrough leadership groups should be closed-end entities, prescheduled to end in three to five years, to coincide with the next full-scale organizational assessment. During those years, the groups' members should go through one rotation of employees. New perspectives and fresh eyes are always needed.

To renew its commitment to the change effort, the organization should revisit the organizational imperative for the inclusion breakthrough. This should be performed periodically, with particular emphasis on enumerating dollars saved and earned. Organizations should also identify success, lessons learned, and how the inclusion breakthrough has enhanced its capability to accomplish its mission and strategies.

REASSESS HOW THE ORGANIZATION'S WORK IS ACCOMPLISHED

The organization should examine all its formal and informal work processes, both internally and externally, not only as a part of a periodic assessment but also as an ongoing process. Individuals and workgroups should constantly evaluate and re-evaluate their practices to make sure they reflect the organization's mission, strategies, values and aspirations for the new culture.

Organization Y was deeply involved in implementing an inclusion breakthrough strategy and saw an opportunity to expand what it had learned beyond the organizational environment to its production processes. Toward that end, the organization formed a rotating-membership group called the Innovation Team, whose mission was to explore ways to dramatically change cycle times, product development methods and the ways in which the organization approached its customers. In the past, the organization had been very siloed, setting up project teams in each division to come up with new approaches from within individual disciplines. Creating an inclusion breakthrough motivated the organization to leverage the different backgrounds and experiences from its various divisions into one team that was diverse in both its functional perspective and the social-identity groups represented.

As a result, the Innovation Team came up with many new and creative approaches to address marketplace challenges by breaking down internal barriers, streamlining various processes, and creating ways to reach out to a diverse set of marketplace needs.

COMMUNICATE ACCOMPLISHMENTS INTERNALLY AND EXTERNALLY

Going public is necessary to maximize the full benefits of the inclusion breakthrough. To attract talented people from the broadest spectrum of backgrounds, having the right stuff is not enough. An organization must also be known as a place of opportunity for growth and success, financially and professionally, with a culture that welcomes people's passions.

To achieve this status, an organization must pursue a course of strategic visibility, seeking to raise public awareness of its workplace practices and accomplishments, especially among the people it wants to attract.

Organization Z had been involved in an inclusion breakthrough strategy for nearly two years, with many successes along the way. Its leaders knew they needed to build on the effort and ensure that new people would bring fresh eyes to the organization. Everyone in the organization was proud of the accomplishments. They knew that even greater things lay ahead, especially if they could inspire their employees and contractors to leverage the organization's recent successes. They also wanted Organization Z to be seen as an employer of choice for in-demand young talent.

Senior leaders realized that the organization needed greater visibility in its efforts and successes. People would not beat a path to their door unless they knew where the door was and what was behind it. So the organization established a Strategic Visibility Team. Following are some of the strategies that the team recommended and implemented:

- Making strong public statements declaring the organization's commitment to an inclusion breakthrough, publicized through public-speaking engagements, newspaper editorials, multimedia press releases, press tours, and article placements—especially in key publications and demographically targeted periodicals that publish annual Best Places to Work lists.

- Issuing strong internal communications, keeping all the people in the organization informed of achievements, ongoing efforts, plans, and decision-making processes to empower current members of the organization as recruitment ambassadors.

- Linking recruitment and retention goals to the mission and business objectives of the organization through internal and external communications.

- Creating and nurturing a strong ongoing presence on college campuses and other key feeder organizations, providing internships, field placements, job-fair presentations, speaking engagements, and informational literature.

- Building mutually beneficial partnerships with business schools and other higher-education institutions.

- Making presentations about Organization Z's successful practices and learnings at key professional and trade conferences.

- Creating a group of new people charged with identifying opportunities for even greater inclusion breakthrough results.

- Serving as a model for successful practices by being cited as *the* organization for other organizations to measure themselves against.

ADDRESS AREAS FOR HIGHER PERFORMANCE

Many organizations are pleased to publicize their best practice policies, recruitment practices, improvement in diversity representation, and other success stories. Such publicity can help earn them favorable mention on Best Places to Work lists compiled by magazines and advocacy groups.

But when it comes to actually creating a welcoming and inclusive environment for all people, the requirements for inclusion on such Best Places to Work lists is abysmally low. Simply offering a generous family-leave policy, a day-care center or referral process, domestic partner benefits, or education subsidies doesn't guarantee that an organization is doing the best it can or meeting the needs of the people in the organization.

To be one of the best organizations in terms of diversity and inclusion policies often means that the organization is just doing better than average.

To be successful in their culture change efforts as well as in their competition for talent, organizations working toward an inclusion breakthrough need to raise the bar, not just on themselves but on their competitors. They need to start announcing not just their isolated success stories but also their highest aspirations. They need to establish the standards to which they want to be held accountable—and then make those standards public so that they *will* be held accountable for them.

Although this might seem like a risky strategy, it is actually a way to take the lead across a range of key business fronts—from winning the competition for talent to becoming an industry's highest-performing organization. By sharing its vision of change, the organization needs to be clear that it is working *toward* this aspiration. It needs to admit that this is unfinished business, without pretending that perfection has been attained, so that people who join the organization see themselves as having a role in creating a new organization and a new vision and do not feel misled into thinking that the work is completed.

As organizations become more and more clear about how to improve their processes, many become even greater advocates for change, joining with other organizations to bring collective clout to issues of social responsibility vital to all organizations. Some become active members of groups such as Business for Social Responsibility or the Social Venture Network so that they can work together to change the way the world does business. Others see that baseline success is not enough and aspire to reach the new baseline

CONTINUOUSLY IMPROVE THE
CHANGE PROCESS

For an inclusion breakthrough to succeed and continue, it must be treated as a process of continuous improvement. Using feedback from ongoing benchmarking and internal surveys, an organization should continually examine and enhance its processes and strategies. The primary assumption should be that strategies and policies must change over time because the needs of the market, the environment, the people and the organization always change.

SUMMARY OF PHASE IV STRATEGIES

Phase IV of the methodology for creating an inclusion breakthrough is really a new beginning to the change process. It is a time for reassessment of the organization's needs, resources, strategies, and competencies—and how well positioned its culture is for leveraging the organization's diverse talents.

It is also a time for renewing the leadership of the change effort, providing new vision, fresh perspectives, and new sources of energy that can come only from a new generation of leaders who stand on the shoulders of those who came before. Although it is a new beginning for the change process, it is not doing the process over. The learnings and experience gained in phases I through III will motivate leaders to take the organization in directions that the leaders of the first phases could not have imagined, predicted, or hoped for.

Breaking Out of the Box

Having read through these chapters, you may be wondering where to start. Often organizations and individuals feel overwhelmed at the task of not only having a program on diversity but also undertaking a major change initiative. At times, a diversity in a box strategy can seem easier to accomplish and manage and clearly easier to get one's arms and resources around. For real, substantial change, however, it is essential to break out of the box and go for a breakthrough. When all is said and done, the question becomes, "How will your (and your organization's) investment of time, money, people, and resources pay off in the long run?" Although quick-fix solutions are appealing, the long-term payoff of an inclusion breakthrough is where the real power of diversity is unleashed.

The first step is to overcome the conceptual trap that an inclusion breakthrough is not possible. You and your organization must be able to dream bold dreams and hold high expectations of what is possible in terms of change.

The second step is to recognize that committing to an inclusion breakthrough strategy and sticking with it is an ongoing challenge. Yet it is one that more and more organizations are undertaking every day. True, the results can be difficult to discern at first. And for many, the journey may seem like a major risk, a leap of faith into the unknown. But the fact that organizations from every facet of society are making steps in this direction speaks loudly. For organizations committed to the journey, achieving an inclusion breakthrough takes bold and radical steps, but it is an attainable reality.

In these pages, we have offered some paths to a breakthrough. Since 1970, our consulting firm has seen dramatic changes in the willingness of many organizations to address diversity. We have experienced the transformation of business units and the blossoming of individuals and work teams. We have seen excitement unleashed as people contribute their wisdom, their voices, and their value. We know that inclusion breakthroughs are possible. And we know that they are not easy.

HOW TO BEGIN

To bring about an inclusion breakthrough in your organization, you have to start by making one within yourself. To lead an inclusion breakthrough effort, you must commit yourself to constant learning and growing. Part of creating a safe environment for growth and change is making it safe for people to experiment and to know that each step informs the next—to allow for mistakes, to deal with obstacles, and to identify new opportunities along the way. It takes both patience and a sense of urgency to achieve a breakthrough: patience to position all the right elements and urgency for execution.

Getting an inclusion breakthrough effort successfully launched may seem like a triumph, but it is really just the first step of the journey. It is a time for celebration, but after that, the real work begins. Just when you think you are making great progress, you may encounter the roughest going. As Kaleel Jamison often said, "Change in the middle looks like failure."

To succeed and survive on this journey, you and others must be committed to the potential of all people in the organization and the positive power of their combined efforts. Above all, you must be brave. As you begin this undertaking, here are a few key lessons we have learned.

DON'T TRY TO DO IT ALONE

Inclusion is a process of partnerships. Find partners who share your commitment to creating an inclusion breakthrough.

You must do more than simply enable others to join you. You must also be willing and able to join them. In a true partnership, you will sometimes lead, sometimes follow and sometimes share both roles at the same time.

There is no singular road to an inclusion breakthrough. Herb Shepard said, "[You need to] light many fires [and] not build hills as you go" (1985). Partnership means developing mutually supportive relationships and learning from each other along the way. You cannot create an inclusive environment alone.

GROW THE CHOIR

The best strategy for creating an organization-wide inclusion breakthrough is to create small-scale working models. Don't waste energy challenging the most difficult obstacle. Instead, work with your partners and allies to create successful models that other people can join or emulate—a pull versus push strategy. Many people dismiss preaching to the choir because they are already on board and supportive of the effort. However, it is critical to enlist those already supportive of change. Find a way to strengthen the power and voice of the choir members as catalysts for change.

WALK TOWARD YOUR TALK

An inclusion breakthrough is a process of discovery, of uncovering opportunities and possibilities that have been buried in the organization. There will always be more things to learn, more ways to enable people to work together more effectively, and more opportunities to explore. Be brave enough to create goals beyond your current capabilities, and then strive to achieve them. Too often efforts fail because people are judging the ways in which behavior does not live up to the espoused values of inclusion and the vision of change. It takes time to truly live the vision of an inclusive culture. The true test is whether the organization and its members are walking toward the talk. Remember, our vision is often ahead of our behavior, so the question is, "How are you closing the gap?"

EXPAND YOUR BOUNDARIES

This work is bigger than any one sector; all are needed. If we don't address the communities in which organizations exist, we would be building on quicksand.

The key to success is the joining of all segments of society. Corporations cannot do this alone, communities cannot do this alone, nor can governments or any organization. It will take all of us partnering together in new ways to make an inclusion breakthrough. A society cannot be healthy, just, and flourish unless all members are included and engaged in making it better.

We can change the world

Our vision is to change the world by changing one organization at a time. Organizations provide the leverage points, the pockets of readiness that can unleash the limitless power of human diversity. We celebrate those of you already on the journey, and we welcome and applaud those of you bold enough to start.

Glossary

The following terms are used throughout this book. The entries provided here are not dictionary definitions, but our conception of what these words mean, the contexts in which we use them, and their relevance to the work of building inclusion and leveraging diversity.

360-degree Vision: The ability to see problems, solutions, opportunities, ideas, and situations from all vantage points. This is one of the benefits of an organization that leverages its diversity. 360-degree vision means that people with a variety of experiences and backgrounds bring a range of perspectives to a problems and opportunities. Monocultural organizations by comparison have a much smaller field of vision.

Ableism: Discrimination based on physical ability. People with physical, mental or emotional disabilities often experience oppression in the workforce and society at large. Our culture favors the so-called able-bodied, even for tasks that can be accomplished equally by someone with a disability.

Affirmative Action: A legal remedy in the United States designed to help correct the historic disadvantage that women and people of color have experienced in society, the workplace, and higher education. Over time Affirmative Action has expanded to address discrimination against other groups as well. See also diversity.

Critical Mass: The portion of the organization's population necessary to create successful change. Also referred to as the "tipping point" (Gladwell, 2000), this represents a far smaller percentage of the organization than most people realize, often around 10 to 15 percent. What's important is that this be the right 10 to 15 percent: formal and informal thought leaders who can make things happen and who have influence over their peers. The American Revolution was supported by less than a quarter of the colonists, but those who did support it were highly effective at creating change.

Discrimination: Actions rooted in prejudice (conscious or unconscious) that serve to put at a disadvantage one person or group based on some characteristic. In society—and in the workplace in particular—discrimination is often based on membership in social identity groups.

Diversity: The range of social identity groups that comprise an organization. The terms diversity, affirmative action, equal employment opportunity, and inclusion are often mistakenly used interchangeably, but each has a unique meaning. See also Affirmative Action, Equal Employment Opportunity, and inclusion.

Equal Employment Opportunity: Laws that collectively prohibit discrimination on the basis of gender, religion, race, color, national origin, age, and physical ability level. See also diversity.

Followership: A necessary skill for successful organizations. Much is written and said about leadership, but leaders can't succeed without good followers. Members of the organization must be willing to partner with leaders, to speak up and provide valuable feedback to them, to trust them, and to coach them.

Glass Ceiling: An unseen barrier that prevents a person from rising above a certain point in an organization. Much has been said about the glass ceiling, particularly as it relates to white women's inability to break into the upper echelons of management. See also sticky floor.

Improvement Metric: Measurement tool that targets specific areas of an organization's procedures, programs, and operations. Many organizations include diversity in their metrics, but define this narrowly as the demographic composition of their workforce. For a more accurate picture, other manifestations of diversity and inclusion must be considered, such as hiring practices, promotions, turnover rates, grade level demographics, succession planning, and performance evaluations. The Improvement Metric captures a greater complexity of variables to ascertain progress beyond mere visible differences.

Inclusion: Fully and respectfully involving all members, regardless of gender, religion, race, color, sexual orientation, national origin, age, or physical ability, in the activities and life of the organization.

Isms: Various forms of oppression and discrimination, such as sexism, classism, racism, heterosexism, ageism, and ableism. These are prejudicial power dynamics that form the basis for privilege and oppression in organizations and in societies at large.

Leveraging Diversity and Inclusion Index: A measure of cultural readiness,–that is, the degree to which an organization's environment is a place where diversity can thrive. The index includes a set of questions that relate to leveraging diversity and creating a culture of inclusion. It provides a broad and quantifiable metric that holds people accountable for achieving higher and higher performance and demonstrates the importance of diversity and inclusion to the organization's bottom line.

Make a Difference Day: Many organizations, large and small, are committed to being socially responsible and supporting their communities. Make A Difference Day is a national event in the United States created by USA Weekend Magazine. Millions of people in the United States volunteer on that day, accomplishing thousands of projects in hundreds of towns and cities and helping an estimated 25 million people each year. In addition to participating in the annual event, many organizations are taking the idea a step further by instituting Make a Difference Days, which are paid days off for community service. For example, our firm, The Kaleel Jamison Consulting Group, Inc., offers all employees two paid days off work per year to serve a community effort.

Monocultural: Having to do with one dominant culture. In monocultural organizations, members of one social identity group set the rules and enjoy the privileges of power; there is one way of succeeding, one style or approach that is valued. Members of other social identity groups may be allowed in, but they must assimilate into that dominant culture or experience resistance and discrimination. This is in contrast with organizations that leverage diversity. In which differences are valued and people from a variety of social identity groups and representing a range of backgrounds, perspectives, and experiences are able to succeed.

Nibbles: Defeating words, actions and beliefs that inhibit people's ability to be their best or to fully contribute their talents and strengths. The term was coined by Kaleel Jamison (1989) in her landmark book The Nibble Theory and the Kernel of Power. Nibbles can come from others who aim—consciously or not—to cut you down or diminish your effectiveness (such as "You are too smart" or "You ask too many questions"). They can come also from within as an expression of self-destruction or low confidence (such as "I'm really not very good at this" or "This is probably not a good idea, but. . .").

One-up/One-down: A system in which one social identity group experiences privilege or power (one-up status) while another is oppressed (one-down). As a result, privilege and oppression are linked, with the success of one group necessitating the failure of another. This dynamic does not allow for true equality or equal opportunity; it instead fosters dominance and subjugation. The two groups often have very different perceptions of privilege, group identity, and the need for change.

Organizational Imperative: The business case for a culture change effort. Becoming more diverse and inclusive is not a nicety; it's a necessity that brings competitive advantage and bottom-line benefits. In an age of global markets and an increasingly diverse workforce, diversity and inclusion are business tools that are needed not only for success but also for survival.

People of Color: An inclusive term that encompasses a wide range of social identity groups, including Asians, indigenous peoples, Latinas/Latinos, and blacks. We use people of color instead of minority because the latter has pejorative connotations and is also inaccurate: People of color comprise the majority of humans in the world.

Performance Scorecards: A workplace tool used to measure people's effectiveness in accomplishing work goals in specific areas such as business results, development of people, customer service, and product development. In many organizations, scorecards provide the critical information upon which promotion, salary, and training decisions are made. They establish the criteria that are considered critical for individual and organizational success, and for which people in the organization are held accountable. As such, it is essential that leveraging diversity and inclusion metrics are included in performance scorecards. They emphasize the importance of these initiatives to the organization's objectives and ensure that people are held accountable and rewarded for learning and demonstrating diverse and inclusive behaviors.

Pinches: A phrase coined by John Glidewell and John Sherwood (1973) that refers to conflicts in an early stage. Left unaddressed, these become crunches—major problems between people that impede their ability to function fully. Pinches are also opportunities for growth and learning if the people involved openly discuss the discomfort they're feeling rather than hide or ignore it.

Pockets of Readiness: Places in an organization that are primed for change. Not every person or division in a large group is equally prepared for or excited about enacting a change initiative. A smart strategy is to find the areas that are likely to embrace and implement change, and then use them to start the process, provide visible examples for the rest of the organization, and propel the change effort for rollout across the organization.

Qualified: Often used as a modifier to describe people of color or women but is rarely used when describing white men. It is often assumed that white men are qualified and that qualified people of color or women are an exception to the rule.

Racial Profiling: The practice of singling out a specific group of people for discriminatory treatment based on some shared social identity characteristic. (Although the term itself mentions race, the same practice may be applied to groups based on other social identity factors.) For example, police engage in racial profiling when they use race to determine which motorists to stop, which passersby to search, and which suspects to draw weapons on. Racial profiling fits the literal definition of prejudice: Its perpetrators "pre-judge" people based on stereotypes and racist attitudes.

A Safe Place™: Safe Place and the Safe Place logo are registered trademarks of EQUAL! at Lucent, licensed to LEAGUE at AT&T. The Safe Place program provides a non-threatening way for managers and employees to make a statement that homophobia and hostility will not be tolerated in the workplace.

Second Class Citizens: People typically disenfranchised by society and made to feel inferior based on their race, gender, ethnicity, sexual orientation, or some other social identity factor.

Separate but Equal: This term was coined in the United States Supreme Court's infamous 1896 Plessy v. Ferguson decision, which gave segregation the legal stamp of approval and helped enable the Jim Crow era. The Court determined that separate facilities, procedures, accommodations, and so on for blacks and whites were acceptable, as long as they were equal. In 1954, the Court reversed itself, acknowledging in its Brown v. Board of Education decision that segregation violated the United States Constitution and that separate can never be equal: The very notion of dividing people based on race guarantees inequality, no matter what the conditions.

Six Sigma: A quality and cost initiative that uses data and statistical analysis to locate and eliminate process errors. A sigma rating determines the number of defects-per-million-opportunities in any manufacturing, service, or transactional procedure. These programs are useful in manufacturing processes but they are not necessarily intended for application to human systems.

Social Identity Groups: The various cultural delineations that help define people's personalities, experiences, perspectives, and social status, as well as other aspects of their lives. In many societies these are typically constructed around factors such as nationality, religion, sexual orientation, race, education level, gender, economic class, physical ability level, parental status, and occupation. Our membership in these social identity groups has a strong effect on who we are and how we are perceived in the world, often determining who experiences privilege and who experiences oppression.

Sticky Floor: Like the glass ceiling, this is a reference to the internal forces of resistance that prevent certain social identity groups from succeeding in an organization. Unlike the glass ceiling, which addresses how high a person can rise, the sticky floor refers to the fact that many women of color and other women are consigned to the lowest levels of organizations, and barriers are in place that prevent them from moving up in the organization despite their talents.

White Women/Women of Color; Women of Color/Men of Color:
Different social identity groups. We separate women of color
from white women and men of color to acknowledge the dis-
tinctly different life experiences of each group. Although all
women do share some traits and experiences based on their common gender, white women typically enjoy much more privilege
than women of color in many Western cultures. Similarly, men of
color and women of color share some experiences based on their
race and ethnicity but also receive vastly different treatment based
on their differing genders. Grouping them ("people of color" or
"women") ignores these differences.

References

——•——

Browne, John. "A Progress Report." 2001 Conradin von Gugelberg Memorial Lecture on the Environment, Stanford University, Stanford, CA, 2001.

Gans, Roger S., Katz, Judith H., and Miller, Frederick A. "Becoming a 'Worthy Organization'." *OD Practitioner*, Fall 1998.

Gladwell, Malcolm *The Tipping Point*. Boston, MA: Little, Brown and Company, 2000

Glidewell, John C. and Sherwood, John J. "Planned Renegotiation: A Norm Setting OD Intervention." In *Contemporary Organization Development: Orientations and Interventions*, edited by W. W. Burke, 35 — 46. Washington, DC: NTL Institute, 1973.

Gray, Elizabeth Dodson. *Patriarchy as a Conceptual Trap*. Wellesley, MA: Roundtable Press, 1982.

Jamison, Kaleel. "Straight Talk: A Norm-Changing Intervention." *OD Practitioner*, June 1985.

Jamison, Kaleel. *The Nibble Theory and the Kernel of Power*. New York, NY: Paulist Press, 1989.

Jensen, Marjane. "Eleven Behaviors for Inclusion." The Kaleel Jamison Consulting Group, Inc., 1995. *

Katz, Judith H. and Miller, Frederick A. "Cultural Diversity as a Developmental Process." *The 1995 Annual, Pfeiffer and Company International Publishers*, 1995.

LaBarre, Polly. "Marcus Buckingham Thinks Your Boss Has an Attitude Problem." *Fast Company*, August 2001, 88.

Shepard, Herb. "Rules of Thumb for Agents of Culture Change." *OD Practitioner*, 1985 (originally published in 1975).

Stum, David. "America @ Work." Study presented at Annual Meeting of Society for Human Resource Management, Minneapolis, 1998.

Vaill, Peter. *Managing as a Performing Art*. San Francisco, CA: Jossey-Bass, 1990.

"Affirmative Action: Myth vs. Reality." Equal Rights Advocates http://www.equalrights.org/affirm/myth.htm

"Amy Domini Receives Leadership In Business Award." 2001 http://www.domini.com/about-domini/News/Press-Release-Archive/index.htm

"Census 2000." http://www.census.gov

"Clean, Green,. . . and Lean." *Tomorrow Essentials*, 2001. http://www.environmental-expert.com/magazine/essentials/mar2001/article1.htm

"Firms Helping with Housing Costs." *The Los Angeles Times Home Edition*, January 28, 2001.

"Learning Community Behaviors." The Kaleel Jamison Consulting Group, Inc., 1987,1998.*

"The Paradox of Diversity." Author Unknown

*Unpublished articles referenced in The Inclusion Breakthrough are available online at http://www.inclusionbreakthrough.com

Index

●

360 degree vision, 19, 73

A

ableism, workforce injustice, 99–100
absenteeism, 56, 64
accountability
    diversity element, 11
    formalizing, 174–175
accountability mechanisms, 93–94
accountability systems, 78
acquisitions, 31
action, timing during culture change,
    155–156
added value, 93
Advisory Council for Diversity and
    Inclusion, 144–145
affinity groups
    defined, 165
    employee network, 79–80
Affirmative Action, 4–5, 101
African American, 60, 70, 82–83, 125,
    129–131
After-hours recreation program, 75
age, policies and practices baseline, 93–94
agents of culture change, purposes,
    158–162, 170, 182
alignment
    building a platform for change, 147,
        149–159
    culture change elements, 34
    network groups and organization's
        bottom line, 167
Americans with Disabilities Act (ADA),
    adherence importance, 91–93
Anglia Water, 118
Asian, 70, 136
Asian Americans, 9, 70, 82–83, 125
associates, organizational capabilities, 66–69
assumptions
    outmoded policies, 76
    racial stereotype, 131

attrition, 58
awareness education programs, 29

B

Bank #1, 22–24
Bank #2, 22–24
Bank of America, 122
barriers
    baseline, age, 93
    Buddy system, 78
    fear of the unknown, 36
    isms, 99
    physical, 92, 143
    "problem-to-be-solved" approach to
        diversity, 12–13
    women, 85–86
    workforce discrimination, 101
baseline benefits, 66, 81
baseline competencies, 53
be brave, 64
"be like leader" model, 12
be like us approach, diversity
    shortcomings, 11–12
benchmarking, 30
benefits packages, policies and practices
    element, 80–81
Bhutan, 50
bisexuals, policies and practices baseline,
    83–85
bonuses, incentives, 76, 107, 112, 167,
    174–177
boulder of oppression, workforce
    injustice, 100–101
Bronx, 3
Brown, Capers, 118
buddy system, advantages, 167
building a platform for change
    education and alignment, 149–150
    identify internal leadership, 153–155
    organizational assessment, 145–149
    organizational imperative, 141–145

building a platform for change *(continued)*
    senior leaders commitment required,
        139–140
    taking action timing, 155–156
building blocks, effective change, 137
business case, 30
buy-in, 102, 143–144, 179

C

Canada, 126–127
carbon dioxide, 118
career development, 83, 165, 175
career-pathing bias, 73
Chamber of Commerce, 68, 121–122
Chief Operating Officer (COO), 90
children, 70, 87, 100–101
classism, workforce injustice, 99–100
clear communications, competency
    element, 62
coaching, 165–168, 183
Coca-Cola, 122
communications
    clarity importance, 62
    free/clear flow, 112
    increasing momentum, 158
    style, 89
community responsibility
    cost considerations, 117–120
    global accountability, 116–117
    greenhouse gas reduction, 118
    inclusion breakthrough element, 44
    investment funds, 119–120
    long-term benefits, 122–123
    meanings, 115–116
    partnerships, 120–122
    volunteerism, 120–122
Company A, 108
Company B, 109
compensation, core business issue, 75
competencies
    11 inclusive behaviors, 59–64
    all members contribute, 63
    authentic greetings, 59–60
    braveness required, 64
    clear communications, 62
    definitions, 53–54
    diverse team building, 50

competencies *(continued)*
    evaluation techniques, 56–58
    external forces, 51
    forms of incompetence, 47–48
    inclusion breakthrough elements, 41–43
    inviting quiet team members to speak,
        63
    listening skills, 61–62
    meeting time considerations, 63–64
    niche marketing, 130
    Organization F re-examination
        example, 64–71
    resolving disagreements, 60–61
    safety, 60
    sharing thoughts/experiences, 63
    team leader's culture challenges, 51–52
    understanding tasks, 62
    workgroup diversity accountability,
        55–56
    workplace requirements, 49–50
competency-based leadership-develop-
    ment process, 181
conflict, resolving, 60–61
continuous improvement, 134
contribution, competency element, 63
Cornell University, 3
critical mass, 83, 86, 130, 151, 158,
    162, 181
cross division/cross-department
    movement, 53
cultural perspectives, 52
culture
    developing individual awareness,
        28–30
    organizational influences, 26–27
    team leader challenges, 51–52
culture of inclusion, 30–34, 36, 38, 159,
    169, 181–182
customers
    expanded view, 133–134
    raised expectations value, 128–129

D

degendering roles/positions, 86
Dell Computer, 122
demographic market segments, using,
    125–128

dependent-care benefits, 175
developing individual awareness, 28
developing leadership, 38
development levels, performance, 28–31
dimensions of difference, 19
disabled persons, policies and practices
    baseline, 91–93
disagreements
    often offer more complete visions, 22
    resolving, 60–61
discrimination
    creating process to address, 164–165
    workforce injustice, 100–101
diversity
    accountability importance, 11
    Affirmative Action, 4–5
    differences in hiring process, 4
    failure to leverage, 6
    flawed assumptions/foundations, 11–14
    Human Resource responsibilities, 5–6
    leveraging benefits, 6–7
    motive importance, 13–14
    "problem-to-be-solved" approach
        barrier, 12–13
    recruiters, 82
    safe workplace environment, 36–38
    senior leaders (dominant groups) view
        toward, 13
    support structure importance, 11
    workforce leveraging, 97–113
Diversity and Inclusion Action Group,
    66–67
Diversity and Inclusion Action Task
    Force, 152
Diversity and Inclusion Index, using,
    173, 175
Diversity and Inclusion Task Force, 121,
    152
diversity efforts, bank merger example,
    22–24
diversity in a box
    defined, 5
    inclusion barriers, 7–8
    moving beyond, 6
diversity programs
    combining into an initiative, 30–31
    implementing, 30

Divisional Inclusion Councils, 160
domestic partners
    benefit policies and practices element,
        81
    discrimination issues, 164–165
dominant culture, 29, 52, 54
dominant groups
    diversity program views, 13
    leveling/raising the playing field,
        14–16
    overcoming undervalued feeling,
        27–28
Domini, Amy, 119
Domini Social Equity Fund, 119
dot-coms, 59, 130
downsizing, 22–23, 110, 178, 180
duplication of effort, 160

E

education
    baseline leveraging diversity, 175–176
    developing inclusion breakthrough,
        172–173
    importance to momentum, 162–164
    sessions, 172, 176, 180
education and alignment, culture change
    component, 149–150
emotional safety, 111
employee networks, policies and practices
    element, 79–80
employees
    authentic greetings, 59–60
    boxing in, 6
    comfort factor outcome on hiring, 10
    free agent mentality, 105–106
    full utilization of skills/abilities, 6
    incentives for success, 174, 176–177
    individual awareness development,
        28–30
    leveling/raising the playing field,
        14–16
    marginalizing, 8
    new hire retention incentives, 167
    survey, 173, 178, 180
    trusted as business partners, 111–112
    valuable resource approach, 18–20
    workplace environment issues, 36–38

employer of choice, 108, 122, 144
enhanced value, marketplace, 125–134
environment
 physical/emotional safety importance,
  111
 safe workplace, 36–38
 safety creation, 60
 serial-employment, 104–105
ethnicity, 4, 9, 127, 173
evaluations, 58, 73, 153
extended-level staff meetings, 91
external forces, new competencies
 challenge, 51

F

facilitators, 168
Fannie Mae, 80
Fast Company magazine, 105
fear, diversity barrier, 36
feedback
 senior leaders, 148–153
 sessions, 153, 156, 160
financial incentives, 76, 81
flavor-of-the-month, 77
flexible work schedules, policies and practices element, 82
flextime, 13, 81–82, 86–87, 107, 175
floating holidays, policies and practices
 element, 81
focus groups, uses, 146–147
followership, 109
Fortune 100, 153
Fortune 500, 59
Fortune, Inc., 141

G

Gans, Roger, 109
The Gay-Lesbian-Bisexual-Transgender
 Alliance, 68
gays, 81, 83–85, 100, 106, 131, 147
Gen Xers, 121
gender, 4, 9–12, 18, 28, 101, 103, 173, 180
Giving Voice sessions, benefits, 147–148
glass ceiling, 85–86, 101
global
 competition, 1, 47, 64

global *(continued)*
 economy, 18
 management, 89
grade distribution, 53
grants, 80–81
Gray, Elizabeth Dodson (*Patriarchy as a
 Conceptual Trap*), 21
Greater Green River, 118
green mutual funds, 118
greenhouse effect, 118
greetings, fellow employees, 59–60
group leaders, 68

H

harassment, 85–87, 100, 163, 177
Harley-Davidson, 80
Harvard Management Update magazine,
 122
hazing, 76, 78, 111
heterosexism, workforce injustice, 99–100
hierarchies, 2
Hindu, 50
hiring, policies and practices, 77–82
hiring practices
 monocultural values, 10
 niche marketing, 131
hiring process, differences, 4
Hispanic Chamber of Commerce,
 122–123
holidays, 76, 78, 81, 89
housing grants, 81
Howard University, 81
Human Resources, diversity efforts, 5–6

I

implementation, 35–36, 151–157,
 159–160, 166
 incentives, 176–177
 inclusion program, 30
incentives, 81, 112, 176–178
inclusion
 acknowledging differences/similarities
  in people, 17
 barriers, 7–8
 human energy increase, 17
 implementing program, 30

inclusion, *(continued)*
  importance of building, 6
  sense of belonging, 16–17
inclusion breakthrough
  11 inclusive behaviors, 59–64
  addressing discrimination, 164–165
  community responsibility, 44
  connecting with senior executives, 26
  creating, 135–137
  defined, 7
  developing long-term plans, 171–174
  elements, 41–45
  formalizing, accountability, 174–175
  implement incentives, 176–177
  importance of, 1
  improving market value, 125–134
  key element alignment importance, 34
  KJCG methodology Phase I, 140
  KJCG methodology Phase II, 158
  KJCG methodology Phase III, 172
  KJCG methodology Phase IV, 185
  linking throughout organization,
    171–172
  marketing choices, 126–128
  mission-critical imperative, 17
  new competencies element, 41–43, 47–71
  niche marketing, 130–131
  partnership with people, 38–39
  performance feedback systems, 177
  policies and practices, 73–95
  policy element, 43
  practice element, 43
  putting plan into action, 178
  short-term plan development, 157
  social responsibility, 44
  view of customers, 133–134
  workforce leveraging, 44
Inclusion Breakthrough Cycle, 126, 136
Inclusion Breakthrough Leadership Team,
    173
Inclusion Implementation Work Team,
    155, 159
inclusive behavior, 58–59, 65, 86, 144,
    147, 150, 156, 165, 174, 181–182
inclusive practices, benefits to business, 177
India, 50
individual awareness, developing, 28–30

Industrial Revolution, 18
initial short-term plan, developing, 157
initiatives, combining with diversity/
    inclusion programs, 30–31
Inovest Strategic Value Advisors, 118
in-service training programs, 75
internal competition, 76
investment funds, socially responsible,
    119–120
isms, effect on diverse workforce, 99–100

J

Jackson, Bailey, 3–4
Jamison, Kaleel, 111
job-for-life, 75
job sharing, 81, 86

K

key competencies, 59
KJCG methodology, inclusion break-
    through tables, 140, 158, 172, 186

L

languages, 4, 19, 50, 52, 76, 89, 130
Latinos/Latinas, 6, 82, 102, 121–122
leaders, putting in lead positions, 25
leadership
    effective change building block, 137
    identify for culture change effort,
      153–155
    group, 54, 154
learning
    community, 163
    effective change building block, 137
learning partners, value to senior leaders,
    150–153
lesbians, 81, 83–85, 100, 106, 131, 147
leveling the playing field, 102
levels, performance development, 28–31
leverage, effective change building block,
    137
Leveraging Diversity and Inclusion
    Improvement Metrics, using, 174–175
leveraging diversity, baseline education,
    175–176
Levi Strauss, 122

linkage, effective change building block, 137
listening skills, competency element, 61–62
low-interest loans, 80

M

Make a Difference Days, 122
management, diversity accountability, 11
Manager Education Session, 69, 163
managers, training source, 175
Managing as a Performing Art (Peter Vaill),
    20
Managing for High Performance and
    Inclusion education program, 163
marketplace
    enhanced value introduction, 45
    increasing organization value, 125–134
    social responsibility, 119
markets
    importance of understanding, 131
    inclusion breakthrough influences,
        126–128
    niche, 129–131
    social-identity-group, 125–128
McDonald's, 20
measurement systems, 79
meetings
    conflict resolution, 61–62
    disagreements offer more complete
        visions, 22
    timing considerations, 63–64
mental ability, 4
mentoring, 10, 13, 30, 32, 50, 53–54, 67,
    70, 80–81, 88, 175–176
mentors, "be like us" approach, 11–12, 168
mergers, 22–23, 31, 101
merit rewards, 73
methane, 118
methodology, 172, 181
    Phase I, 140
    Phase II, 158
    Phase III, 178
    Phase IV, 185
Michigan's Council for World Class
    Communities, 117
mission-critical imperative, 54, 157
misunderstandings, resolving, 60–61
Mobil, 116

Mobil diversity forum, 116
momentum
    agents of culture change, 158–162
    communication, 158
    education to maintain, 162–164
    networks, 165–168
    pockets of readiness recognition,
        168–169
monocultural values, organization short-
    coming, 9–10
morale, 17, 37, 53, 71, 119, 178
mortgage/rental assistance, 81
mothers, niche group, 129
motive, diversity program importance,
    13–14
multiracial identity, 82
Muslim, 50

N

nationalism, workforce injustice, 99–100
nationality, policies and practices baseline,
    89–90
networks
    benefits, 165–168
    employee affinity groups, 79–80
    groups, 79, 81, 165
    inclusion and diversity use, 166–168
new competencies
    11 inclusive behaviors, 59–64
    all members contribute, 63
    authentic greetings, 59–60
    braveness required, 64
    clear communications, 62
    definitions, 53–54
    diverse team building, 50
    evaluation techniques, 56–58
    external forces, 51
    forms of incompetency, 47–48
    inclusion breakthrough element,
        41–43
    inviting quiet team members to speak,
        63
    listening skills, 61–62
    meeting time considerations, 63–64
    niche marketing, 130
    Organization F re-examination
        example, 64–71

port structure, diversity importance, 11
vey questionnaire, 146

ent
    competing for, 18–20, 109–113
    pool, 122, 127, 174
    redefining, 18
    retaining, 18–19, 109–113
ent magnet, 18
ks, understanding, 62
m leaders, 50–51, 53
m members, 103, 109, 111, 164
ms
    all members contribute, 63
    inviting quiet members to speak, 63
    meeting time considerations, 63–64
    sharing thoughts/experiences, 63
amwork skills, 13, 46, 49, 101, 178
chnology, 79, 107
ecommuting, 13
lerance, 99, 153
morrow Essentials magazine, 118
aining programs, 75, 175
ansgendered, 68, 84,–85
o-way agreement, 108
o-way mentoring, 87–88

nderutilized resources, 46

cations, 20
ill, Peter (*Managing as a Performing
    Art*), 20
enting, 118
ivendi Universal, 119
olunteerism, community and social
    responsibility, 120–122
olunteerMatch Corporate, 122

ay of Life model, 29
hirlpool, 117

white men
    networks, 167
    policies and practices baseline, 87–88
Whitwam, David, 117
women's issues, policies and practices
    baseline, 85–87
work assignments, outside-of-work
    responsibility considerations, 22
work contracts, two-way agreements,
    108–109
workforce
    bidding war effect, 106–107
    boulder of oppression, 100–101
    clearly stated roles, 112
    discrimination barriers, 101
    free agent mentality, 105–106
    free/clear communication flow, 112
    high-turnover reasons, 103–104
    leveraging diversity, 97–98
    magnet for talent traits, 109–113
    power and effect of isms, 99–100
    racial profiling, 102
    redefining talent, 18, 109–113
    retention strategies, 105
    reverse discrimination, 102
    serial-employment, 104–105
    trusted as business partners, 111–112
    turnover by length of employment,
        106
Workforce Culture Team, 164–165
workforce leveraging, inclusion break-
    through element, 44
workplace, safe environment importance,
    36–38

X

Xerox, 80

Y

Yale University, 81

Z

Zero Tolerance for Harassment, 153
zings, 111

new competencies (*continued*)
    resolving disagreements, 60–61
    safety, 60
    sharing thoughts/experiences, 63
    team leader's culture challenges, 51–52
    understanding tasks, 62
    workgroup diversity accountability,
        55–56
    workplace requirements, 49–50
new human frontier, 21
niche marketing, partnerships, 132–133
nibbles, 111
niche markets, 125, 129–131
Nike, 122
Noto, Lou, 116–117

O

older workers, policies and practices
    baseline, 93–94
one-down group, 90, 99
one-off activities, diversity and inclusion,
    175–176
one-up group, 88, 99, 101
one way investments, 117, 123
oppression, 21
Organization A, overcoming racial
    discrimination, 31–34
Organization B, recruitment practices,
    50
Organization C, competence definitions,
    53–54
Organization D, workgroup diversity
    accountability, 55–56
Organization E, competency evaluations,
    56–58
Organization F, competency
    re-examination example, 64–71
Organization G, performance-
    appraisal/career-pathing bias, 73–75
Organization H, cultural identity
    recognition, 78
Organization I, rewards/scorecard
    example, 79
Organization J, unable to address isms,
    102–103
Organization K, misunderstanding
    high-turnover, 103–104

Organization L, workforce diversity
    benefits, 107–108
Organization M, strategic volunteerism
    example, 121–122
Organization N, marketing expansion
    choices, 126–128
Organization O, focus group with
    mothers, 129
Organization P, diversity advantage, 130
Organization Q, organizational
    imperative, 141–145
Organization R, Giving Voice focus
    groups, 147–149
Organization S, inclusion breakthrough
    implementation, 155
Organization T, inclusion breakthrough
    plan, 159–1162
Organization U, discrimination issues,
    164–165
Organization V, networks linked to
    business objectives, 166
Organization W, inclusion breakthrough
    implementation, 173–174
Organization X, inclusion breakthrough
    implementation, 178–183
organizational assessment, culture change
    component, 145–149, 156, 159
organizational blindness, 12
organizational capabilities, 64–67, 171
organizational change, 25
organizational hierarchy, policies and
    practices baseline, 90–91
organizational imperative, culture change
    component, 141–145, 159
organizations
    Affirmative Action misconceptions,
        4–5
    becoming a talent magnet, 18–19,
        109–113
    capitalizing on diversity, 1–2
    community and social responsibilities,
        115–123
    culture influences, 26–27
    decision basing criteria, 9
    disregard for differences, 4
    diversity accountability, 11
    diversity in a box, 5–6

organizations *(continued)*
  employees as valuable resource, 18–19
  engaging people's differences, 21
  enhanced market value, 125–134
  growth/development opportunity
    importance, 110
  inclusion barriers, 7–8
  inclusion breakthrough elements, 41–45
  individual awareness development,
    28–30
  leveling/raising the playing field, 14–16
  monocultural values, 9–10
  motive behind diversity effort, 13–14
  moving beyond diversity in a box, 6
  new talent introduction versus
    promoting from within, 4
  positioning leaders to lead, 25
  sense of community, 111
  smorgasbord of programs approach to
    diversity, 13
  transitory entities, 19–20

P

Paradox of Diversity, described, 3
parental leave, policies and practices
  element, 81
participation rates, 54
Partnering for Change Team, 179–180
partnerships, 115, 123–124, 127
  community and social responsibility,
    120–122
  diverse marketing strategy, 132–133
  network groups, 177
Patriarchy as a Conceptual Trap (Elizabeth
  Dodson Gray), 21
"pay for expectations", 93–94
people of color, policies and practices
  baseline, 82–83
people-related policies, tying to organization's business challenges, 28, 30
performance
  development levels, 28–31
  feedback systems, 177
  management, 174
  ratings, 54
  review, 66
performance appraisal systems, 70, 73, 79

permanent white water, 20, 22
person of color/people of color, 73, 80, 82
phase I, 119, 156, 162, 171–173
phase II, 157–158, 169, 175
phase III, 172, 176–178, 183
phase IV, 136, 185, 190
philanthropy, community and social
  responsibility, 120–122
physical ability, 4, 12, 28
"pinches", 61
platform for change
  education and alignment, 149–150
  identify internal leadership, 153–155
  organizational assessment, 145–149
  organizational imperative, 141–145
  senior leaders commitment required,
    139–140
  taking action timing, 155–156
pockets of readiness, defined, 168
policies and practices
  age related issues, 93–94
  benefits packages, 80–81
  disabled persons, 91–93
  domestic partner benefits, 81
  employee networks, 79–80
  enacting changes, 77
  flexible work schedules, 82
  floating holidays, 81
  hiring, 77–82
  inclusion breakthrough element, 43
  lesbians/gays/bisexuals, 83–85
  member's outside responsibilities, 110
  nationality issues, 89–90
  organizational hierarchy, 90–91
  outmoded assumptions, 76
  parental leave, 81
  people of color issues, 82–83
  performance appraisal systems, 79
  performance appraisal/career-pathing
    bias, 73–75
  redefining fairness, 94–95
  rewards, 70
  scorecards, 79
  soft policy types, 75
  white men, 87–88
  women's issues, 85–87
practices, versus policies, 43

preferred employer, 67–68
process-improvement initiatives, 72
"problem-to-be-solved" approach,
  diversity barrier, 12–13
product development, 85, 110, 129–130,
  142
professional/career development, 156
profit margins, 142
profit-sharing, 112

R

race, 173, 180
racial profiling, societal injustice, 102
racism, workforce injustice, 99–100
Rainbow/PUSH, 128
recognition programs, new competencies,
  73
recruiting, 85, 93, 104, 166
re-engineering, 31
religion, 4, 18, 35
rental subsidies, 80
resistance points, 162
retention, 23, 52, 55, 77, 82, 105–106,
  165, 167, 174–177
reverse discrimination, excluded member
  charge, 102
rewards, 64, 112
  benefits of new behaviors, 176–178
  policies and practices element, 79
role models, diversity shortcomings, 11–12
roles, clearly stated, 112
Russell Sage College, 81

S

safety
  competency behavior, 60
  workplace environment issues, 36–38
San Francisco Unified School District, 81
San Juan Basin, 118
scorecards, policies and practices element,
  79
senior executives/leaders
  addressing culture challenges, 51–52
  change positioning, 34–35
  commitment to change required, 139–140
  competency definitions, 53–54
  feedback, 148–153

senior executives/leaders (
  learning partners valu
  positioning leaders to
  realizing the truth, 35
  recognizing/dealing w
  recognizing pockets o
    168–169
  rotating people from
  safe workplace enviro
    responsibility, 36–
  worthy of respect/foll
    109–110
sense of belonging, inclus
  16–17
serial-employment, 104
Severn Trent, 118–119
sexism, workforce injustic
sexual orientation, 4, 12,
Sikh, 50
six sigma, 142
skills
  distribution, 54
  identifying needs, 175
social responsibility
  cost considerations, 1
  global accountability,
  greenhouse gas reduct
  inclusion breakthroug
  investment funds, 119
  long-term benefits, 12
  meanings, 115–116
  partnerships, 120–12
  volunteerism, 120–12
social-identity groups
  marketing opportunit
  shopping practices, 12
socioeconomic status, 4
Sri Lanka, 50
stakeholders, involving, 1
sticky floor, 86, 101
stock of choice, 66
stock options, 112
stockholders, 37
straight talk, 32, 145
strategic alliances, 31
succession planning, 104
support networks, 13, 93

About the Authors

———— • ————

Frederick A. Miller is the President and CEO and Judith H. Katz is the Executive Vice President of The Kaleel Jamison Consulting Group, Inc. (KJCG), one of the nation's largest and most respected consulting firms specializing in leveraging diversity and building inclusion. Since 1970 KJCG has been partnering with the leaders of Fortune 500 companies, non-profit organizations, educational institutions, and governmental agencies to make meaningful and sustainable change that benefits people, organizations, and communities.

Noted as one of the forerunners of corporate change in The Age of Heretics, Fred helped pioneer one of the nation's first corporate-level diversity and inclusion efforts in 1972 as a manager with Connecticut General Life Insurance Company (now CIGNA). He joined KJCG in 1979, where his experience has included groundbreaking work in strategic culture change initiatives with public and private organizations. Fred is particularly respected for his ability to examine a system, issue, or culture (small group, community, or organization) at multiple levels and quickly translate his observations into a customized, strategic vision and change-inducing action. Fred is a former board member of the American Society for Training & Development, Ben & Jerry's Homemade Inc., and the Organization Development Network.

Fueled by her passion for addressing systemic oppression, Judith brings more than twenty years of experience to her work in strategic culture change. She helps clients achieve long-term, sustainable change by connecting business strategies (including initiatives for quality, leadership, empowerment, and teamwork) to efforts that leverage diversity and create a culture of inclusion. Judith serves on the board of directors for the Social Venture Network and has previously held board positions with the Organization Development Network and the NTL Institute for Applied behavioral Science. Her first book, White Awareness: Handbook for Anti-Racism Training (University of Oklahoma Press, 1978), remains a landmark in the field.

The authors are frequent presenters at national conferences and publish regularly in magazines and journals.

The authors can be contacted by visiting www.inclusionbreakthrough.com.